CW01657429

SELL £250K ON AMAZON IN 18 MONTHS

MASIMBA RUPANGA

Copyright © 2024 Masimba Rupanga

All rights reserved.

ISBN: 978-1-3999-8974-9

SELL £250K IN 12 MONTHS ON AMAZON © 2024 by
Masimba Shingai Rupanga.
All rights reserved. No part of this book may be used or reproduced in any form or by any means—electronic, mechanical, photocopy, recording, scanning, or other—except for brief quotations, critical reviews or articles without the publisher's prior written permission.
Published by Press Release 42.
Graphics designed by Masimba Rupanga
Printed in the United Kingdom.
FIRST PRESS RELEASE 42 PAPERBACK EDITION
PUBLISHED IN 2024

ABOUT THE AUTHOR

Born in Zimbabwe and now living in Kensington, London, Masimba Rupanga is a dynamic entrepreneur with a flair for fashion design, art, and cycling. His journey began at the age of 17 with selling fabrics in Tanzania, and evolved into launching successful consumer brands on Amazon, achieving over £250k in sales within the first 18 months. His ventures have ranged from transport to tech, showcasing adaptability and perseverance, including a swift pivot during the COVID-19 crisis.

Masimba's entrepreneurial spirit was kindled by his parents. As a teenager, he accompanied his father on overnight train trips from Harare to Bulawayo to purchase shirts for resale—a practice he later mirrored by trading mobile phones between Harare and Johannesburg when he was 18. This foundation of commerce and resilience propelled him to complete his A-Levels in one year, despite facing setbacks.

The loss of his father at 15 saw his mother step up as the family's breadwinner, with Masimba supporting her by sewing school uniforms during school holidays. This early exposure to business fundamentals, even before he understood working capital management, laid the groundwork for his future endeavours.

Masimba's professional acumen extends to senior finance roles; he has served as Group Financial Controller, Head of Group Reporting Finance Transformations, Controller, and Reporting Manager, among other positions, for prominent UK-listed giants like Reckitt Benckiser and IG Group. His expertise was honed as an Audit Manager at Ernst & Young in London, and managing prestigious clients such as British Airways and O2, further solidifying his credentials in finance.

CONTENTS

INTRODUCTION

Let's address the elephant in the room—why would I write a book about selling on Amazon when I'm an active seller myself? Isn't that inviting more competition? The truth is, competition is an inevitable part of business, especially on a platform as vast as Amazon. By sharing my insights, I'm not just opening the door to potential rivals; I'm also contributing to a thriving, competitive marketplace where innovation and quality rise to the top. And let's not forget, Amazon's pie is enormous; there's enough for everyone to have a piece. So, why not monetise my expertise? After all, a more vibrant marketplace benefits us all. With that weight off my shoulders—let's get stuck in.

This book will help you build a profitable startup, selling on Amazon, and I will break down the steps I used to grow my e-commerce startup, with my unique brand, to reach over £250k in revenue in 18 months. I will also provide examples, starting with identifying profitable products currently being sold on Amazon, selling the same under your brand and competing for a cut of the profits. It's going to be challenging but rewarding!

The book includes tips—to help you avoid the mistakes I made, so that you can keep your costs under control and retain much of your profits. I currently sell on Amazon.co.uk. However, the steps and strategies in this book can be applied to other Amazon Marketplaces—for example: amazon.com for the US market or amazon.de for the German market.

"Small new sellers and manufacturers can challenge big, established ones, thanks to the ease of selling goods online. However, the reality is we aren't just in a race to get our products to the market; we're also in a race to communicate why our customers need those products in their lives. Even if we have the best product in the marketplace, we'll lose to inferior product if our competitor's offer is targeted and communicated more clearly"— Donald Miller, "Building A Story Brand"

Throughout the book, I recommend third parties ("suppliers" and "contractors") I have worked with. These businesses do not pay me, and I am not advertising for them. I am telling you who they are to help save you time. If you know suppliers/contractors who offer better value, go with your choice.

I have also included a Glossary of terms ("GOT") at the end of the book. If you bump into any Amazon jargon/acronyms that you are unsure of, check the GOT for definitions.

Let's get stuck in.

1 SELLING ONLINE

The shortest time you might take to start selling on Amazon as a private-label seller is five months. On average, it takes about eight months to make a sale. The diagram below illustrates the key processes and milestones that you and the third parties ("contractors") that you will contract have to complete before launching your first product:

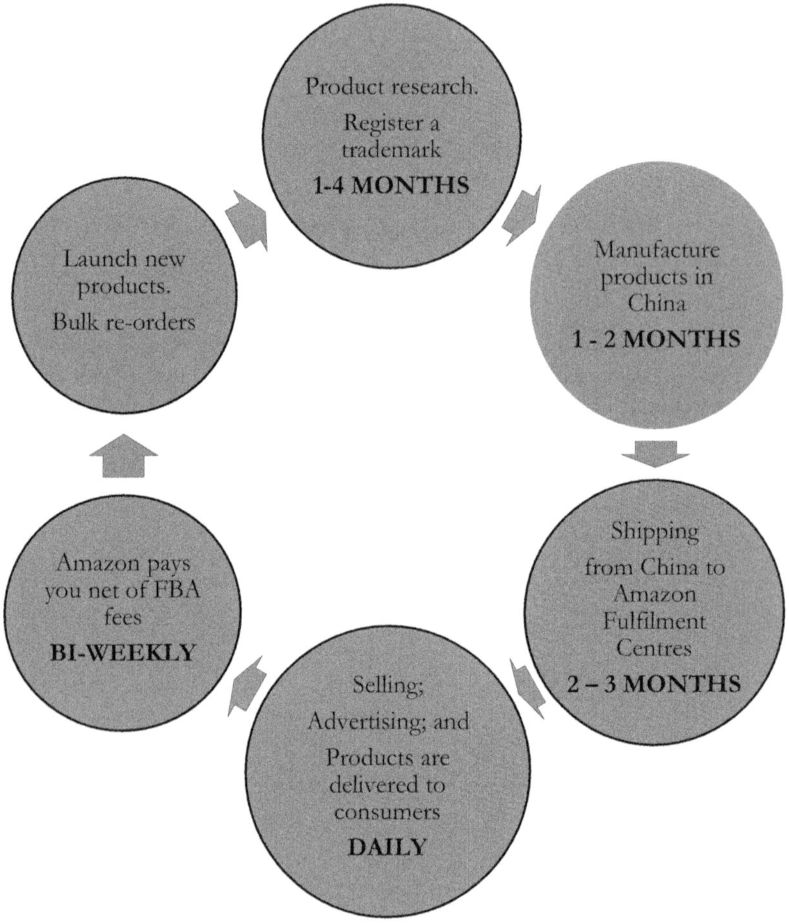
Product research.
Register a trademark
1-4 MONTHS
Manufacture products in China
1 - 2 MONTHS
Shipping
from China to Amazon Fulfilment Centres
2 – 3 MONTHS
Selling;
Advertising; and
Products are delivered to consumers
DAILY
Amazon pays you net of FBA fees
BI-WEEKLY
Launch new products.
Bulk re-orders

"It's no secret, at Amazon, we obsess over customers. And our customers want a trusted destination where they can purchase a wide variety of goods—which is what makes sellers like you so important. We're always looking for ways to add value for our customers and be Earth's most customer-centric company. As an Amazon seller, you take part in offering those customers better selection, better prices, and a top-notch customer experience"—Amazon.

The Amazon Advantage

When you start selling on Amazon, you become part of a retail destination home to sellers of all kinds, from Fortune 500 and UK's large, listed companies to artisan vendors who make handcrafted goods. They all sell on Amazon, for a reason—to reach the hundreds of millions of customers who visit Amazon to shop.

"More than half the units sold on Amazon are from independent sellers; (2) —nearly 60% of Amazon's multichannel sellers named Amazon as their fastest-growing channel; and (3) —over half of Amazon's multichannel sellers prefer Amazon for customer acquisition"—Amazon Internal Data

Why is Amazon Right for You?

Selling on Amazon allows you access to Amazon's customers, including their most loyal Amazon Prime customers. The cost of accessing this market is low. The largest household brands sell on Amazon, as do the emerging brands that will pop on your radar soon. SMEs thrive on Amazon, accounting for more than half the units Amazon sells worldwide. However big your business is, Amazon can help you grow it, as it is the fastest-growing online sales channel.

Selling Vehicle, Business and Selling Models

You can sell on Amazon through a limited company, for example—an LLC in the US, or as self-employed ("sole trader")—that's what I am referring to as the selling vehicle in the diagram below. The business model—the Fulfilment by Amazon ("FBA") model—is what you can use to sell products on Amazon, using your brand, which is also referred to as the "private-label" selling model.

In this book, I will explain other business and selling models, but emphasise the FBA and private label through a limited company model—which I recommend.

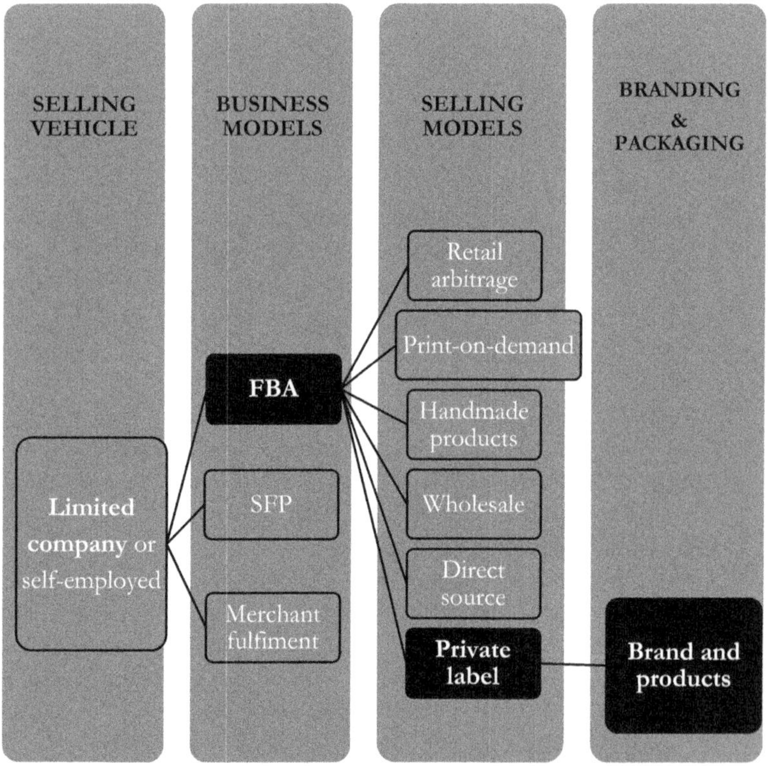

FBA and SFP are eligible for the Amazon Prime Badge. See "Prime Badge" in the Glossary of Terms.

What You Will Do vs What You Will Outsource

The diagram below illustrates the work I completed myself under the heading "In-house", and what I paid third parties to do for me under the heading "Outsourced". You can use this as a guide for what you can outsource:

A trial order is a sizable order placed with the manufacturer to test out the market before a much bigger order—a bulk order.

How Do I Start Selling?

To start selling as a private-label seller, you need the following: (1) product to sell (obviously), (2) a brand name for the product; (3) an Amazon selling account; and (4) a selling vehicle.

For a selling vehicle—you can use a limited company that owns the brand name or as self-employed. A person is self-employed if they run their business for themselves and take responsibility for its success or failure. In the UK, self-employed workers do not have the rights and duties of an employee. They are not paid through pay as you earn ("PAYE")—this means self-employed people take full responsibility for paying the right amount of tax to HRMC through self-assessment. Meanwhile, employees pay taxes and national insurance via their employer through PAYE.

2 PRODUCT RESEARCH

After this chapter, you should be able to pick products to sell on Amazon. Picking the right products will enable you to scale your startup quicker with lower advertising spend—the latter usually makes up a big part of your operating costs. This chapter is split into two sections: (1) Primary research: the research that you will complete using Amazon, and (2) secondary research: which you will complete using other tools, for example: Google, Instagram, You Tube and Facebook.

Before we jump in—for every product that you will shortlist, you must place it in one of these categories for further analysis:

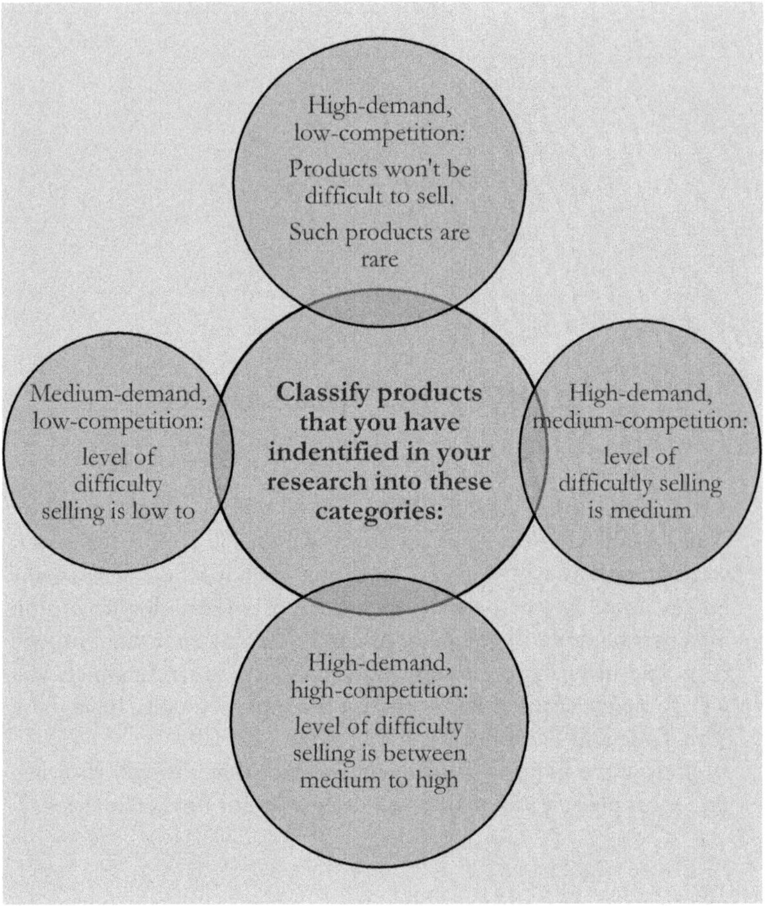
High-demand, low-competition:
Products won't be difficult to sell.
Such products are rare
Medium-demand, low-competition:
level of difficulty selling is low to
Classify products that you have indentified in your research into these categories:
High-demand, medium-competition:
level of difficultly selling is medium
High-demand, high-competition:
level of difficulty selling is between medium to high

Focus on products that you have classified in the high-demand and low-competition category. They are hard to find but they exist. You should be able short list a few in one to two months.

High-demand, medium-competition and high-demand, high-competition products are also good; however, they will need a lot more investment in customer acquisition and advertising.

For medium-demand and low competition products, while it may initially not be hard to sell in this category, it will become hard to grow and scale your business as there is a limited number of customers due to a shallow market depth. Generally, products on Amazon have low margins, so you will end up with very little or no profit if you can't sell large volumes.

Primary Research

The best place to start your product research is on Amazon itself: www.amazon.co.uk. You can identify products with high demand from the number of product reviews. Generally, customers only leave product reviews if the product or service is exceptional, or when something has gone wrong, and the customer wants to make a complaint. According to Amazon, 10% to 20% of customers leave feedback. In my experience, five to ten in every 100 customers leave a product review. Therefore, a product with, for example, 10,000 reviews and multiple sellers also with thousands of reviews, demonstrates greater market depth and high demand. When there is high demand for a product on Amazon, you can also get a piece of the action if you have a high-quality listing and you run ads—I'll say more on product listings and advertising later in the book. Do not let sellers with thousands of reviews intimidate you into thinking you can't compete with them even though you will be starting out with few reviews.

In addition, there are strategies and programs that Amazon has put in place to ensure that new products and new sellers get product reviews and feedback—further details are in the Customer Reviews chapter.

The fact is that Amazon wants new sellers to succeed; their business model and growth plans are based on being able to enrol new sellers and customers. Hence, Amazon keeps rolling out the red carpet for new sellers with various incentive programmes and free advertising offers in some marketplaces for a period.

Now, let's drill in to identifying products to sell—refer to the screenshots on the following pages, for examples. Then access amazon.co.uk and click on the main menu—this will take you to the different shopping departments and categories.

16:32
◄ Search
Search Amazon.co.uk
Grocery
In-Store Code
Alexa Lists
Deliver to London W14 8
7 ways to unbox a saving with us
Find out more
Kindle Scribe
Amazon Devices
Original Peloton Bike | Indoor Stationa...
£1,345.00 prime
PELOTON
Sponsored
Deals for you
0

For each department, drill down into the various categories and sub-categories. For example, under "Devices & electronics", drill down into Electronics for further subcategories.

Keep drilling into the sub-categories until you hit the bottom category and click "Best Sellers". Then look at the number of reviews for the top 100 sellers. Calculate the average number of reviews per product and rank your products and sub-categories, accordingly, based on their actual number of reviews.

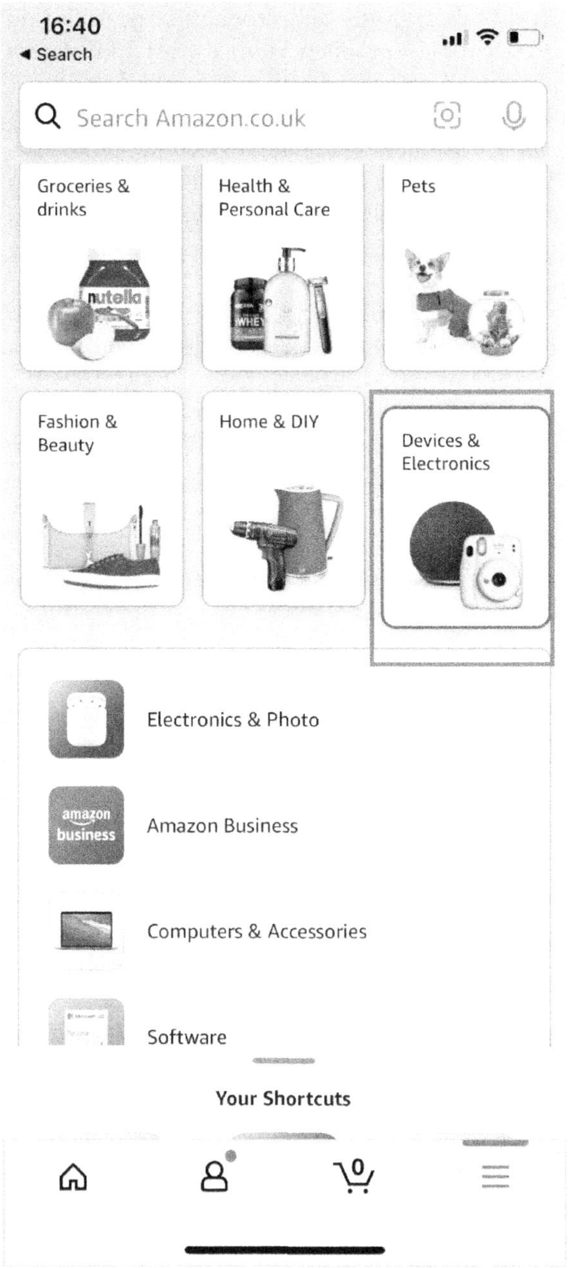
16:40
Search
Search Amazon.co.uk
Groceries & drinks
Health & Personal Care
Pets
Fashion & Beauty
Home & DIY
Devices & Electronics
Electronics & Photo
amazon business
Amazon Business
Computers & Accessories
Software
Your Shortcuts
0

Go through as many subcategories and products as possible and produce a list of your top 10 products from at least 10 different categories in high demand. For those products, establish:
(1) How long they have been listed on Amazon.
(2) The average annual number of product reviews per product—this is calculated by dividing the total number of product reviews by the years the product has been listed on Amazon. This is to weed out products with unusually high reviews due to having been listed for longer.

As a rule of thumb, if a product has about 2,000 reviews a year, on average, you can assume the seller sells 20,000 units a year. This is calculated as 2,000 reviews divided by 0.1, on the assumption that only 10% of customers leave reviews.

Suppose there are 10 sellers for that product, all with an annual average of 2,000 reviews. In that case, yearly market demand is 200,000 units, calculated as— 2,000 reviews divided by 0.1 x 10 sellers.

Do more analysis and ask yourself if there will be growth in that category. For most categories on Amazon, there will be considerable growth in the next few years due to the ongoing shift from physical stores to online. Don't get me wrong—I am not saying that there is going to be a total wipe-out of the high streets, shopping malls and retail parks—in fact, some retailers with little online presence, such as Primark, Target, Costco and Dollar General, are expanding their physical presence and, in recent years, have reported record sales.

However, for most physical store retailers, unless they improve their online presence and delivery capabilities, for example: "by beating next day delivery", they don't stand a chance against Amazon—Amazon has more resources and a 20-year head start in logistics.

"Amazon's constant innovation gives it a huge competitive advantage, which many retailers will struggle to match. Too many physical stores lack the strategy and efficient logistics that might help them thrive in retail's new 'online' era. Their biggest issue is that they still rely on customers coming to them to choose their purchases, whereas their rivals deliver".—The Economist (2017), "Stores are being hit by online retailing"

If you find a product with a market that can grow organically in the next couple of years, that's great; if not, it's a question of how hungry you are to compete with other sellers for a piece of the action through effective advertising, procurement and cost management. Are you willing to work harder and faster than your competition? These differentiating factors will enable you to offer prices that beat the competition and still make a profit. On Amazon, most of the products look similar—that's because they come from the same group of manufacturers. It's mainly the brand names that are different. Therefore, customers look for two things: price and number of reviews—reviews are the social proof and confirmation that the product will do what it says on the tin.

Let me ask you this: if 10 people—based on 10 reviews, tell you that a product works and the price is excellent, will you not buy it? If yes, does that mean 10 reviews are good enough? According to Amazon's research, 15 is the magic number. To get 15 reviews, you must sell at least 150 to 200 units, which is not such a tall order. As a new seller, you can sell your first 200 units at a price slightly lower than the competition to get the first 15–20 reviews quicker… and Bob's your uncle!

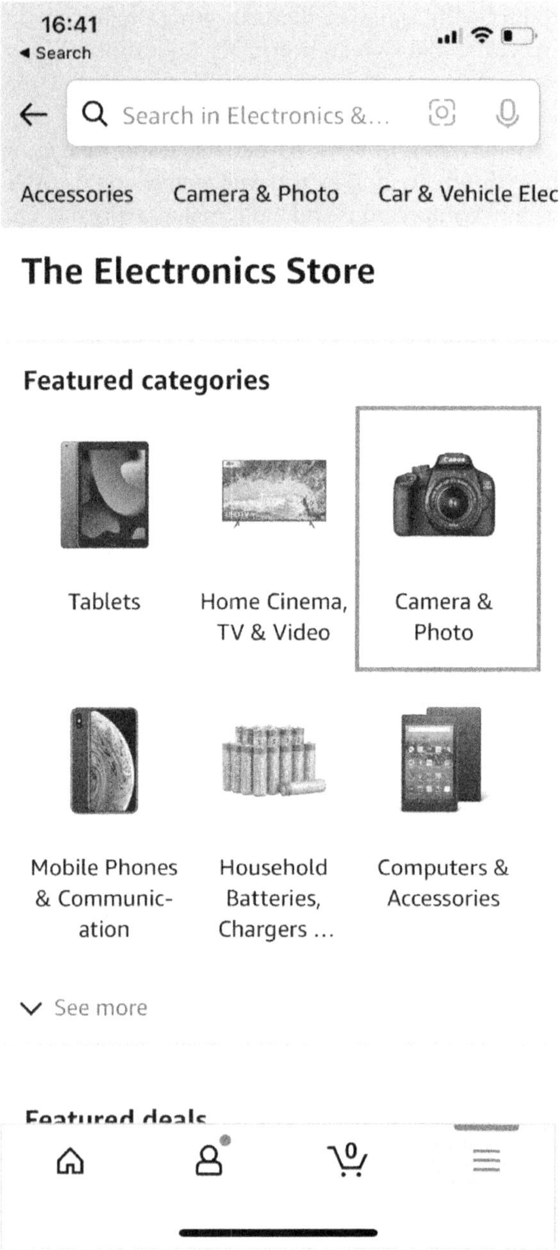
16:41
◂ Search
Search in Electronics &...
Accessories
Camera & Photo
Car & Vehicle Elec
The Electronics Store
Featured categories
Tablets
Home Cinema, TV & Video
Camera & Photo
Mobile Phones & Communic-ation
Household Batteries, Chargers ...
Computers & Accessories
See more
0

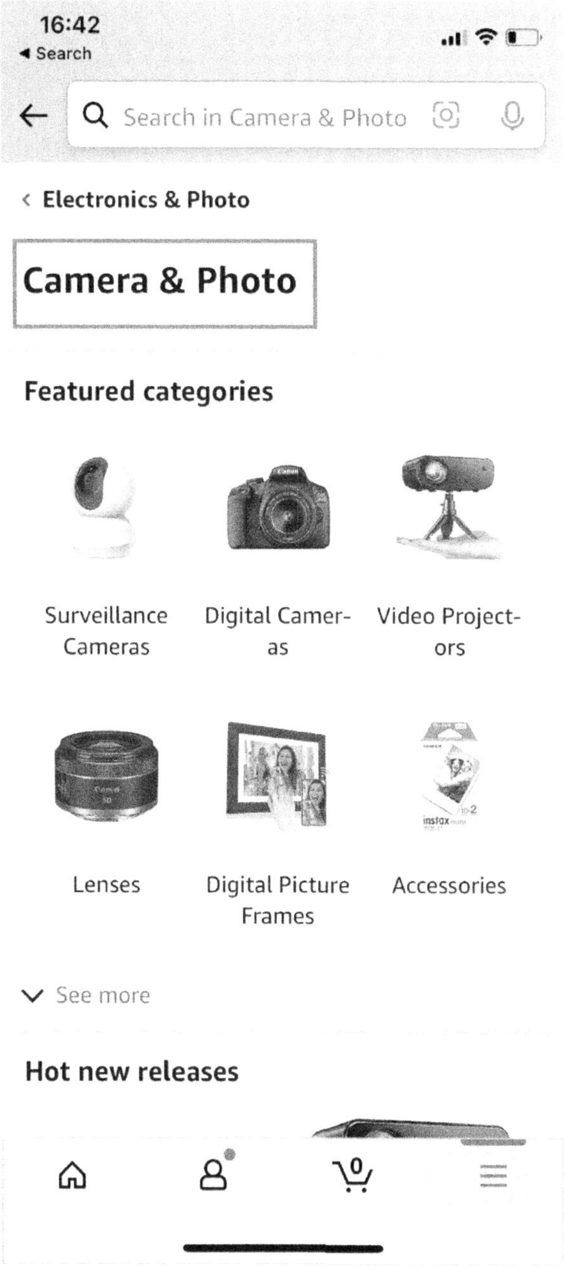
16:42
◂ Search
Search in Camera & Photo
‹ Electronics & Photo
Camera & Photo
Featured categories
Surveillance Cameras
Digital Camer-as
Video Project-ors
Lenses
Digital Picture Frames
Accessories
See more
Hot new releases
0

Scroll down to the "Best Sellers" section.

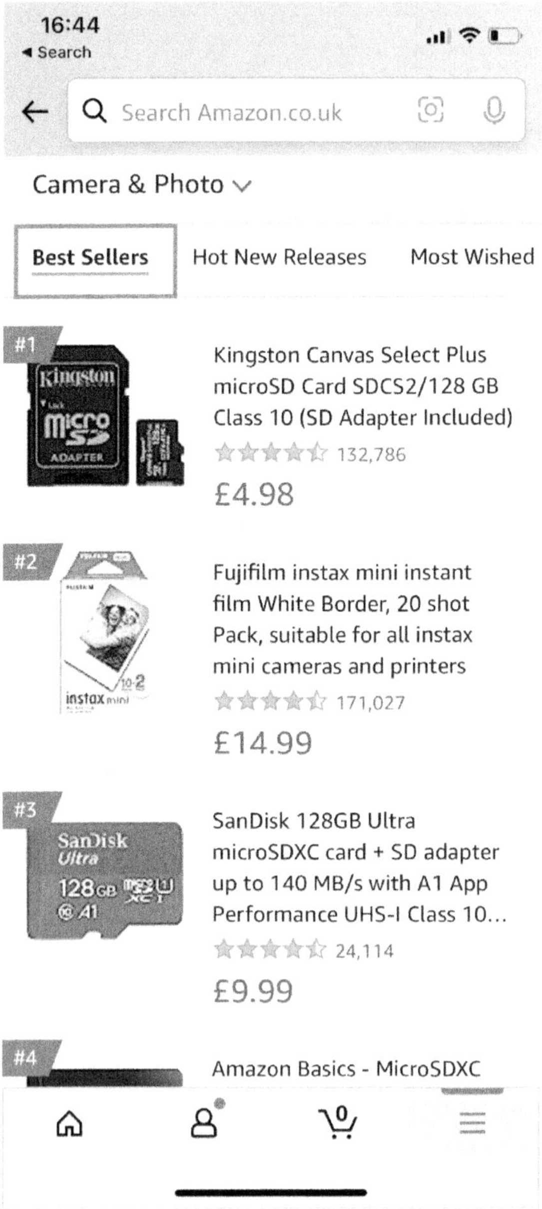

You can determine the number of reviews per product from the product pages. For example, see the screenshot below.

16:47
◂ Search
Search Amazon.co.uk
AKASO EK7000 4K30FPS Action Camera - 20M...
£59.99 prime
Sponsored
Visit the Heegomn Store
3.8 230
Heegomn Waterproof Digital Camera for Children, Full HD 1080P, 8x Digital Zoom, 16MP Underwater Cam for Teenagers/Beginners (Red)

You can determine the period a product has been listed on Amazon using the "Date First Available", which can be obtained by scrolling down the product pages under "Product information"—for example, see the screenshots below.

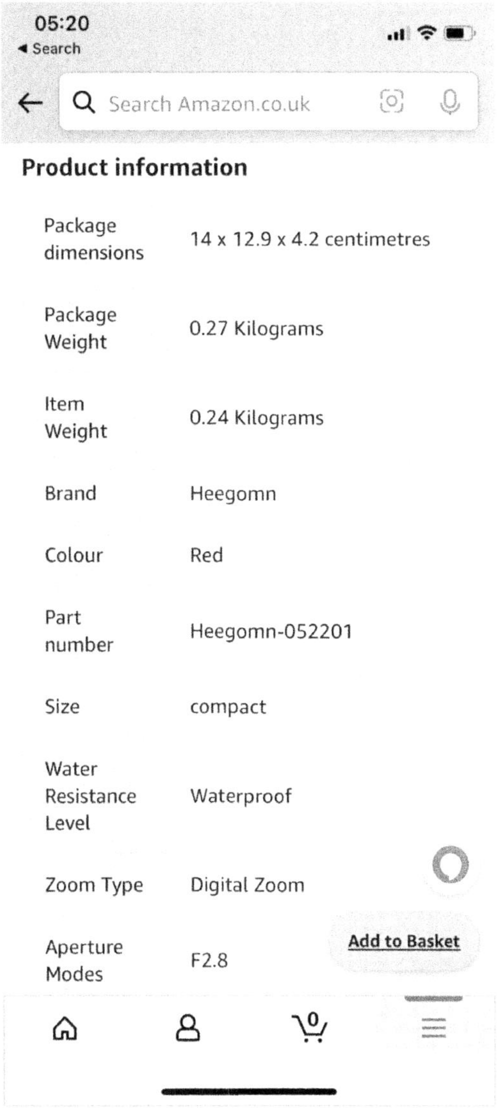

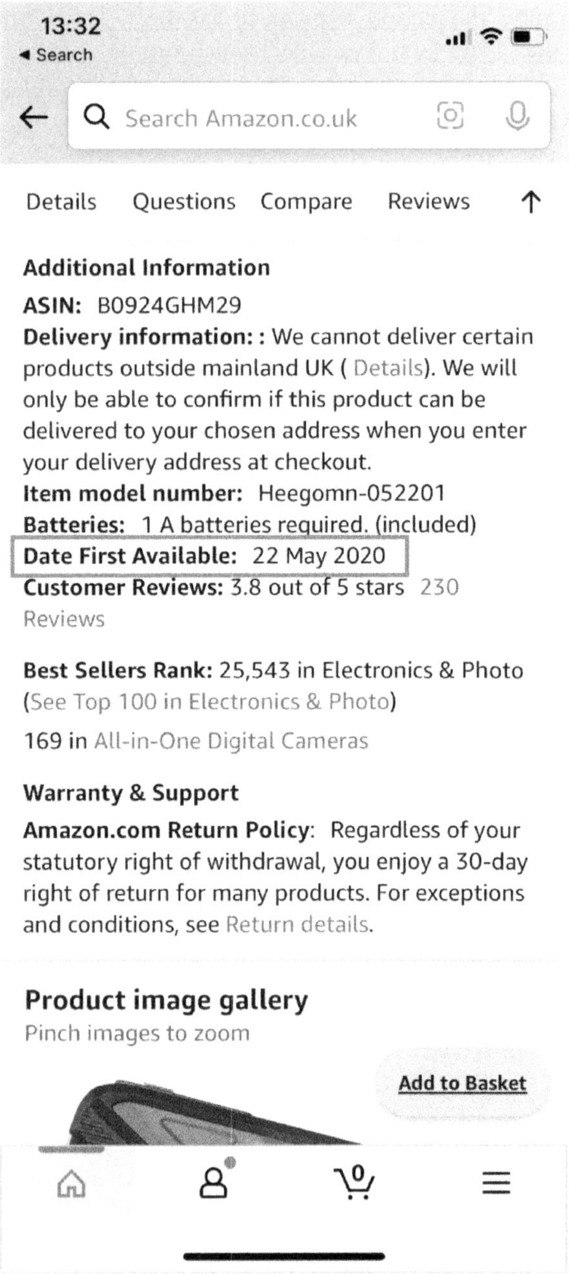
13:32
Search
Search Amazon.co.uk
Details
Questions
Compare
Reviews
Additional Information
ASIN: B0924GHM29
Delivery information: : We cannot deliver certain products outside mainland UK (Details). We will only be able to confirm if this product can be delivered to your chosen address when you enter your delivery address at checkout.
Item model number: Heegomn-052201
Batteries: 1 A batteries required. (included)
Date First Available: 22 May 2020
Customer Reviews: 3.8 out of 5 stars 230 Reviews
Best Sellers Rank: 25,543 in Electronics & Photo (See Top 100 in Electronics & Photo)
169 in All-in-One Digital Cameras
Warranty & Support
Amazon.com Return Policy: Regardless of your statutory right of withdrawal, you enjoy a 30-day right of return for many products. For exceptions and conditions, see Return details.
Product image gallery
Pinch images to zoom
Add to Basket
0

Deciding which product to sell is not a purely formulaic process, but here are some guidelines and product characteristics to help you decide what to sell:

(1) Existing solid demand;

> Ensure you understand who your target market is—a well-defined target market will reduce your ad spend, as you will know the exact keywords to use to reach this market. For example, if you're selling kids' toys, your ads will target kids directly, who will do an excellent job of nagging their parents on your behalf to make a purchase. Meanwhile, if you're selling kids educational products, you may want to target the parents directly—unless the kid you are targeting is like my "weird" 13-year-old niece who uses her pocket money to buy books—which is probably representative of about one kid in every 10,000.

(2) Mass consumption—consider "repeat purchase" products. Many household goods are repurchased time and time again. Targeting products that apply to most age groups, genders, income levels, individuals, businesses, local customers, and national and international buyers increases your target market. Therefore, select products that fit into most of these categories. However, selling internationally is not child's play. Start by focusing on one country, preferably the one you live in or whose language you understand best, for at least 18 months before you start selling in other countries. In my first year, I was excited to be selling in Italy and France; it was not so exciting when the reviews started pouring in—for example, customers asking why their product had a 3-pin plug and why the manual was not in Italian/French. You probably think I should have seen this coming—yeah, sure, maybe. Schoolboy error, right? However, with so much work to do before you can make a sale, it's easy to make such mistakes.

(3) Low to medium competition;

(4) High margins—generally, pricier products have higher margins. Target products with a selling price above £30 and go as

high as you like if there is proof of high demand. Products that have low prices end up with little to no profit. Always remember that Amazon wants a certain minimum amount for every order.
(5) Target products with no legal issues, and that aren't highly technical and complex—unless you have experience working with such products.

> If you have the right experience, knowledge, and confidence—go for it. Keep a balance; products that are too easy to produce will face a lot of competition compared to complex products. I regret not launching my first product because it needed special approvals from Amazon —it was a digital scale with a lithium battery, which would allow customers to record weight details through a cloud-based App and enable customers to analyse the data over time. Today, I see other sellers who are doing well in that category. Therefore, constantly challenge yourself and ask yourself this, "Is this too easy or too complex? Even though it sounds complicated, will I pull it off?" If you think you can pull it off, don't hesitate.

(6) Small and light products—as above, most small products don't command a high price. Ensure you strike a balance between size and value. Use the FBA calculator (see page 32) to determine if your product will be profitable at competitive prices. Amazon offers reduced fulfilment costs for products eligible for the FBA Small and Light programme—eligibility is determined using price, weight and size. Search "FBA small and light enrol" in Seller Central for details or, on the main menu, click on "Growth", followed by "Explore programmes", and finally, click on "Small and Light".

(7) Stick to hard-to-break items—it's not uncommon for products to break while in transit, so select products that are unlikely to break.

(8) Products that can be improved easily—products with a lower review rating have the potential for improvement, giving you a unique selling point if you can find a manufacturer who can make the necessary improvements.

(9) Low seasonality—products with lower seasonality will ensure a consistent level of sales month on month and can make managing your working capital easier. On the contrary, my most profitable product, which also has the highest annual sales is seasonal. Bear in mind that some lenders—for example, Uncapped who used to offer loans you would repay based on your sales performance—do not like to fund working capital on seasonal products—in 2022 they told me that I might struggle to keep up with repayments during quieter months. Natwest came to the rescue.

(10) Long product life—some non-perishable, usually high-tech, products may have short sales windows, say 18 months. For your first product, I would advise that you go for a product that won't become outdated too fast.

If you are still trying to figure out ideas, check out Jungle Scout (https://www.junglescout.com), who claim they will show you profitable products. They will provide you with their "Amazon add-on" software, a Chrome/Firefox extension that can estimate the monthly sales units for products listed on Amazon. It's a good start. However, I have used their Chrome extension, comparing its results against my actual performance and concluded it is not very accurate.

Customer Questions

For products you plan to launch, go through the questions that customers have asked— they can highlight areas where improvement is needed. Products that need fitting and installation will have more after-sales questions, which is great for customer engagement and building brand loyalty.

Customer questions can be found next to the product title when you are on Amazon on a desktop, and after product descriptions when on the Amazon mobile App.

When you are preparing your product listing, use the bullet points and product descriptions to answer customer questions—answering these in advance will make their purchasing decisions easier.

To improve brand loyalty, Amazon recommends responding to customers within 24 hours. You therefore have to make time for after-sales support. Not to worry, it's not very time consuming—it can all be done from your desktop/the seller App. This will include issuing refunds and confirming product guarantees and warranties. You can ask Amazon to destroy/donate products that have been returned for a small fee. This can save you time and costs if the returns are minimal.

Secondary research

When completing your product research, use other platforms like YouTube, Instagram and Facebook. Also, exploit Google tools such as Google Trends and Google Market Finder.

Keyword testing—use Google Trends to determine the popularity of the keywords you want to use in your product listing. Refer to the SEO chapter.

3 FULFILMENT BY AMAZON ("FBA")

This chapter is split into the following sections:
(1) Seller Central—the web portal you will use to manage your Amazon seller account.
(2) FBA Costs and Benefits
(3) FBA Revenue Calculator—a tool you can use to determine the actual costs and profit you will make. I have included an example for a product listed on Amazon.

(1)—Seller Central ("SC")

Your Amazon selling account is managed through Seller Central ("SC")—Google "amazon uk seller central". Sellers can monitor their Amazon sales performance through the SC website. Think of SC as your go-to resource for selling on Amazon. It's the "control panel" to managing your Amazon startup—using it, you can keep track of your daily sales, update product prices, communicate with buyers, review account health, manage payments, add new products, update your listings, and contact seller support.

Go Mobile—use the Amazon Seller mobile App ("Seller App") to do everything listed above, including capturing, and editing professional quality product photos from your mobile phone. In other words, the Amazon seller App is seller central optimised for mobile.

Amazon has two selling plans, individual and professional. You can think of them as standard and premium. At the time of print, the individual plan was £0.75p per item sold, and the professional plan was £25.00 per month—no matter how many items were sold. If you are serious about selling on Amazon, go for the professional plan. You can change plans free of charge, at any time. To complete your registration for a professional selling account, make sure you have access to the following information: (1) your bank account number and sort code/routing number/branch number; (2) chargeable credit card or debit card; (3) government-issued ID, for example, your passport or driving licence; (4) mobile number; and (5) tax information—if you are planning to sell on amazon.com but live outside the US, you will have to complete a form called the W-8BEN, with details such as your name, address and date of birth.

Details about the selling plans:

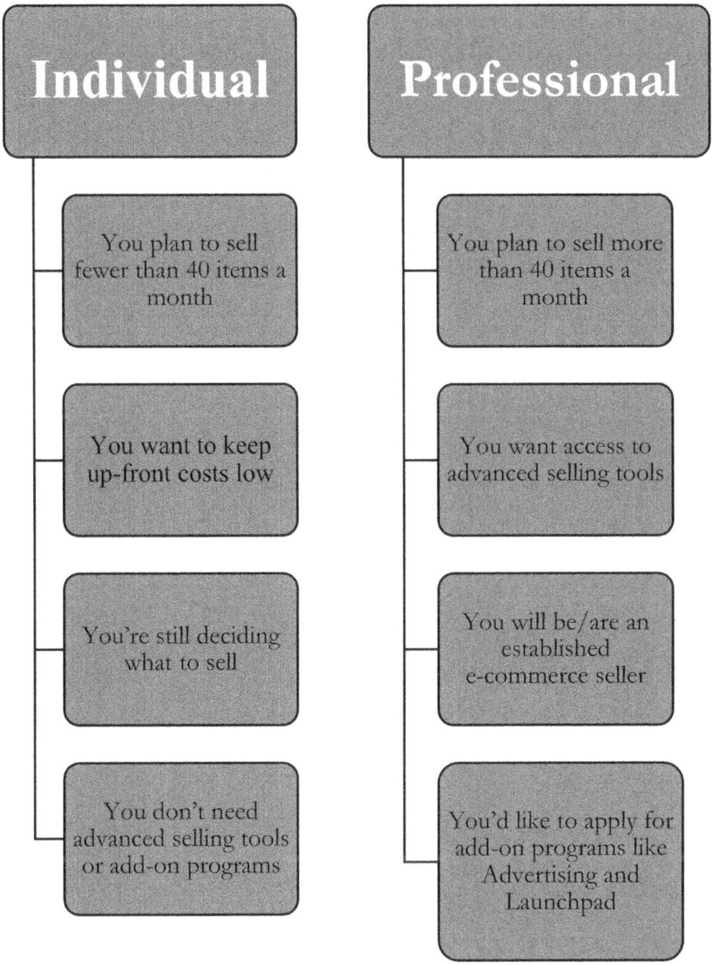

The strategies in this book are for sellers who plan to sell through the professional account.

(2)—FBA Costs and Benefits

There are two options for sellers to get their products to customers: (1) Merchant-fulfilment—your products will be listed on Amazon, but they will be shipped from your warehouse to the customer or (2) FBA, which ships from Amazon Fulfilment Centres ("AFCs") to the customer.

Each method has its benefits, and you must decide which suits your startup. In this book, we will focus on FBA—the least expensive method for entrepreneurs who want to start selling on Amazon without logistics headaches.

FBA Fees

Your selling fees depend on your product category and the optional Amazon programmes you enrol in. Full details of these optional programmes can be found in Seller Central; under the main menu, click "Growth", followed by "Explore programmes". Fees are mandatory, variable or optional. Advertising costs such as cost-per-click ("CPC"), which help promote your product listing, are an example of optional and variable. Below are examples of the most common mandatory and variable fees.

Mandatory and variable fees	
Selling fees	(1) These fees are charged per item sold, and they include referral fees and variable closing fees (2) Referral fees are like a commission, a percentage of the selling price; they vary depending on your product's category (3) Variable closing fees—these apply only to media categories.
Shipping fees	When you fulfil orders yourself, Amazon shipping rates do not apply. Amazon charge these shipping rates based on the product category and shipping service selected by the customer. Amazon recovers these fees directly from customers; therefore, they won't have an impact on your profit.
FBA fees	FBA fees are for order fulfilment, storage, and other optional services such as gift wrapping. There are two types of FBA fees: (1) Fulfilment fees, which are charged per unit sold and include picking and packing your orders, shipping and handling, customer service, and product returns (2)Inventory storage fees, which are charged monthly and are based on the volume held by Amazon for you.
Storage	(1) Storage fees are based on the daily average volume for the space your inventory occupies in FCs starting at £0.40 per cubic foot—at the time of print. (2) The fee per cubic foot/metre varies based on the calendar month: it is lower from January to September, and a slightly higher amount is charged during the high-traffic months from October to December. The exact amount depends on your product category and its size. There is a separate fee structure for the storage of items that are classified as hazmat or dangerous goods.

The Benefits of FBA

"On average, sellers see a 20-25% increase in sales after adopting FBA"—2021 Amazon Small Business Empowerment Report

Amazon has more than 175 fulfilment centres ("FCs") worldwide, which contain more than 150 million square feet of storage space. With FBA, you get to store your products on those shelves. You also get Amazon's world-class customer and returns services, along with other advantages, like automatic Amazon Prime eligibility (see "Prime Badge" in the Glossary of Terms), which can help you scale your startup fast. Amazon sellers can sell to individuals ("B2C") and business customers ("B2B") at no additional cost. I have noticed that there are business customers who buy my products on Amazon and sell them on eBay. Don't be shocked when you see your products being sold on other websites. It used to bother me at first—I think now I have just stopped caring. Outside of Amazon there is not much that you can do to control these resellers.

How FBA Works

Step 1: ship your products in bulk to Amazon, where they will be scanned and made available for sale.

Step 2: with each order, Amazon packs and ships the product directly to the customer.

Step 3: Amazon collects payment from the customer and pays you every two weeks. You can ask Amazon to pay you earlier at no extra charge, but only after your products have been delivered to customers. Getting paid earlier can alleviate cashflow issues. In the UK, it usually takes three to four business days for the funds to reach your bank account from the time you request payment.

Step 4: Amazon's customer service team will handle customers' queries, returns, and refunds. You will have to handle customer queries yourself if the customer contacts you directly.

(3)—FBA Revenue Calculator ("calculator") or ("FBA calculator")

Using the calculator—a live online tool, armed with details of similar products listed on Amazon, you can preview how much your FBA costs and profit will be.

You can enter your total expected sales volumes to estimate your total proceeds, check per-unit-sold estimates, and compare the fees and profitability between different fulfilment methods. The FBA Calculator can be accessed through Google by searching for "FBA Revenue Calculator UK". You can change the search to "...US" or "...Germany", depending on the country you plan to sell in. The calculator is also available in the Seller App.

You can jump straight to the Sourcing chapter—which will help you determine the cost of the product you want to sell and include that cost in calculating the overall profit that you will make selling on Amazon. If you do, you can come back to this section after completing the Sourcing chapter. Alternatively, you can continue reading, make an estimate of what your product will cost to manufacture and later update your profit calculation after you have finalised your manufacturing costs.

The best way to calculate the FBA fees for products you plan to launch is to use ASINs of similar products on Amazon. Alternatively, you need details of the size, dimensions and weight—obtain these details from your manufacturer through Alibaba.com. Refer to the Sourcing chapter. Every product offered for sale on Amazon gets an automatically generated ASIN (Amazon Standard Identification Number), which is different from a Global Trade Item Number ("GTIN") or Stock Keeping Unit ("SKU"). Multiple sellers may offer the same ASIN.

The ASIN can be obtained from the product's detailed pages. The screenshot below shows an example—you can find this under the: "Additional Information" section of the product pages.

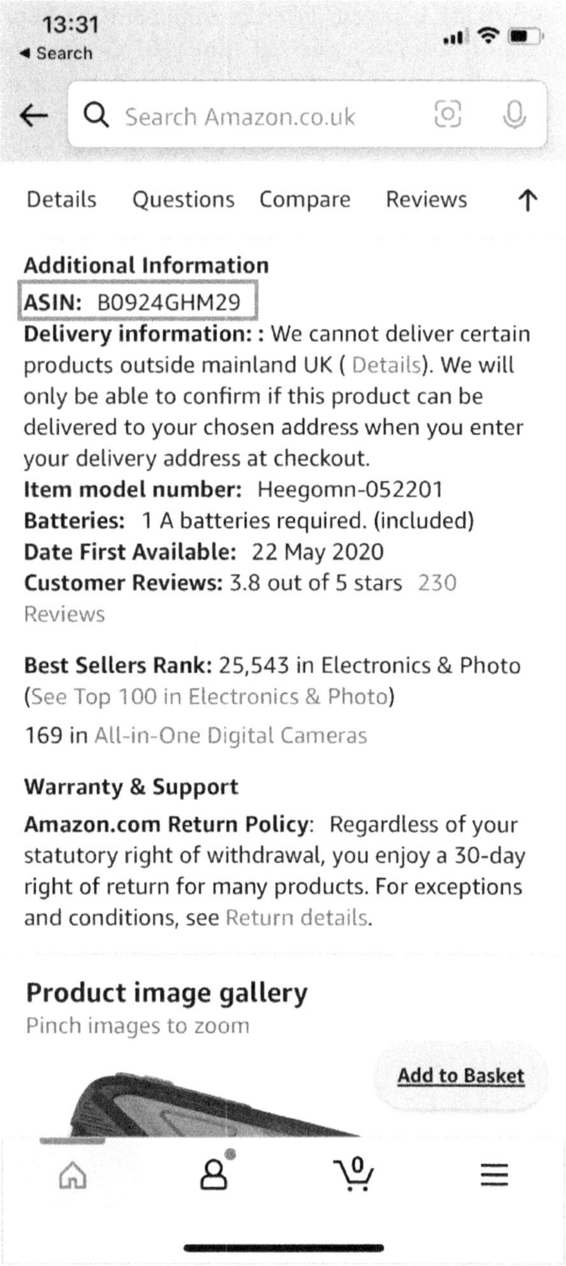

13:31
◂ Search

Search Amazon.co.uk

Details Questions Compare Reviews

Additional Information

ASIN: B0924GHM29

Delivery information: : We cannot deliver certain products outside mainland UK (Details). We will only be able to confirm if this product can be delivered to your chosen address when you enter your delivery address at checkout.

Item model number: Heegomn-052201

Batteries: 1 A batteries required. (included)

Date First Available: 22 May 2020

Customer Reviews: 3.8 out of 5 stars 230 Reviews

Best Sellers Rank: 25,543 in Electronics & Photo (See Top 100 in Electronics & Photo)

169 in All-in-One Digital Cameras

Warranty & Support

Amazon.com Return Policy: Regardless of your statutory right of withdrawal, you enjoy a 30-day right of return for many products. For exceptions and conditions, see Return details.

Product image gallery

Pinch images to zoom

Add to Basket

Using the ASIN "B092GHM29", as above, the screenshots below are results of the calculator—from the Seller App, as of November 2022:

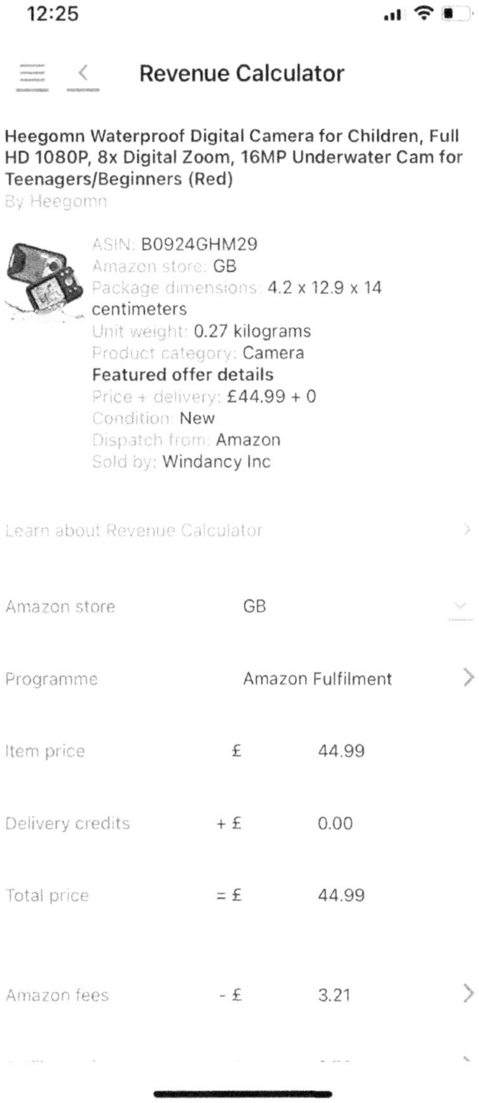

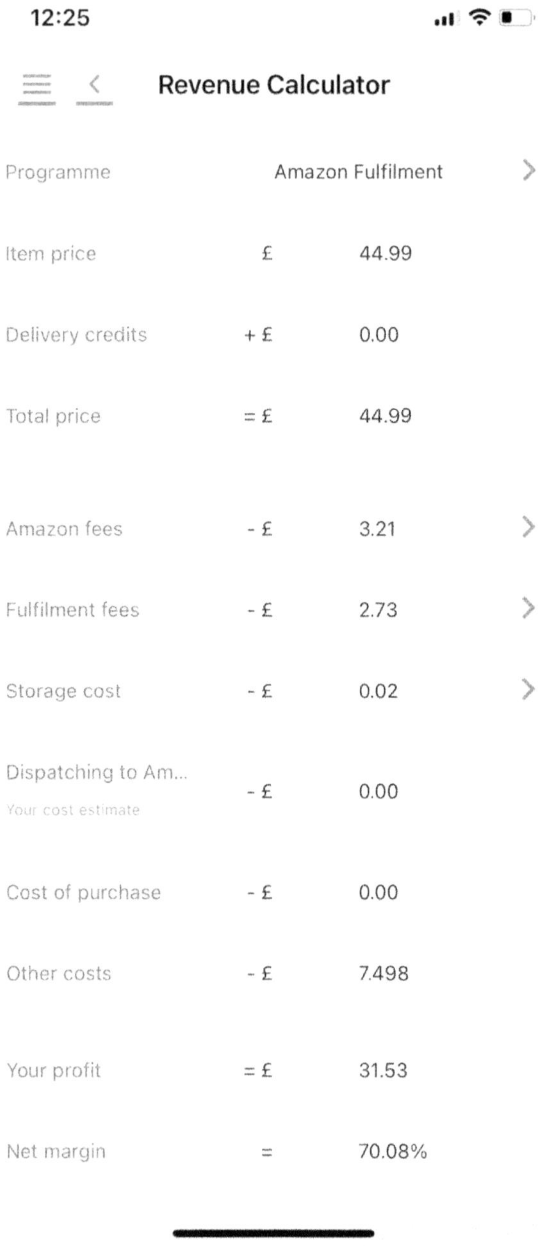
12:25
Revenue Calculator
Programme
Amazon Fulfilment
Item price £ 44.99
Delivery credits + £ 0.00
Total price = £ 44.99
Amazon fees - £ 3.21
Fulfilment fees - £ 2.73
Storage cost - £ 0.02
Dispatching to Am...
Your cost estimate
- £ 0.00
Cost of purchase - £ 0.00
Other costs - £ 7.498
Your profit = £ 31.53
Net margin = 70.08%

If you change the selling price on the calculator, the profit and the related charges will also be updated. Use the Calculator to determine your best offer price based on your target profit margin.

Let's assume that, excluding VAT, the cost of manufacturing a unit is £10.00, shipping is £1.50, customs VAT and duty per unit is £1.30 and the net profit per unit is £4.31. This will result in an overall net profit of £28,723 if you sell £250k worth. See the analysis below for details:

	1 unit £ Per unit	Units	6,670 units £
Selling price/Revenue ("Sales")	44.99	6,670	300,083
VAT at 14%	(7.50)	6,670	(50,014)
	37.49	6,670	250,069
Target ACOS	**20%**		
FBA and selling fees per unit:			
Amazon fees	(3.21)		
Fulfilment fees	(2.73)		
Storage cost	(0.02)		
Total FBA and selling fees	**(5.96)**		
Manufacturing and shipping costs			
Manufacturing	(10.00)		
Shipping	(1.50)		
Customs VAT and duty	(1.30)		
Total cost of manufacturing	**(12.80)**		
Total COS	**(18.76)**	6,670	**(125,129)**
Gross profit	18.73	6,670	124,940
Gross margin	50%		50%
Amazon advertising	(9.00)	6,670	(60,030)
Non-Amazon storage	(2.10)	6,670	(14,007)
Courier—from UK warehouse to Amazon's fulfilment centres	(0.67)	6,670	(4,469)
Accounting, tax, and consulting	(0.62)	6,670	(4,135)
Other administration costs	(0.15)	6,670	(1,001)
Product research, photos and promotions, samples, listings, etc.	(0.45)	6,670	(3,002)
Total operating and administrative costs	**(12.99)**	6,670	**(86,643)**
Profit before tax	5.74	6,670	38,297
Taxation at 25%	(1.44)	6,670	(9,574)
Net profit	4.31	6,670	28,723
Net margin	**11%**		**11%**

"ACOS" is an abbreviation for Amazon advertising cost of sales.

If you are launching your product using the Amazon Launch Pad Programme, you need to add the additional cost—5% of total revenue.

Key performance indicators ("KPI")—for your startup, these can include:
(1) Gross profit;
(2) Net profit; and
(3) ACOS.

Gross profit is calculated as follows:
Sales less cost of sales = gross profit;
Cost of sales mainly comprises landed costs and FBA fees;
Landed costs include the total cost of manufacturing all units + freight costs + customs charges.

Landed costs are incurred in order to get your products to a point where they are ready to be sold ("available for sale") to customers. For an FBA seller, this will be the total costs incurred to get your products into FCs. Your landed costs will not include overheads, such as long-term storage fees.

4 SELLING VEHICLES/SELLING MODELS

In this chapter we will go through the selling vehicles—limited company vs. self-employment and other selling models, which are different to the FBA model we covered in the last chapter. The diagram below shows the different types of business and selling models.

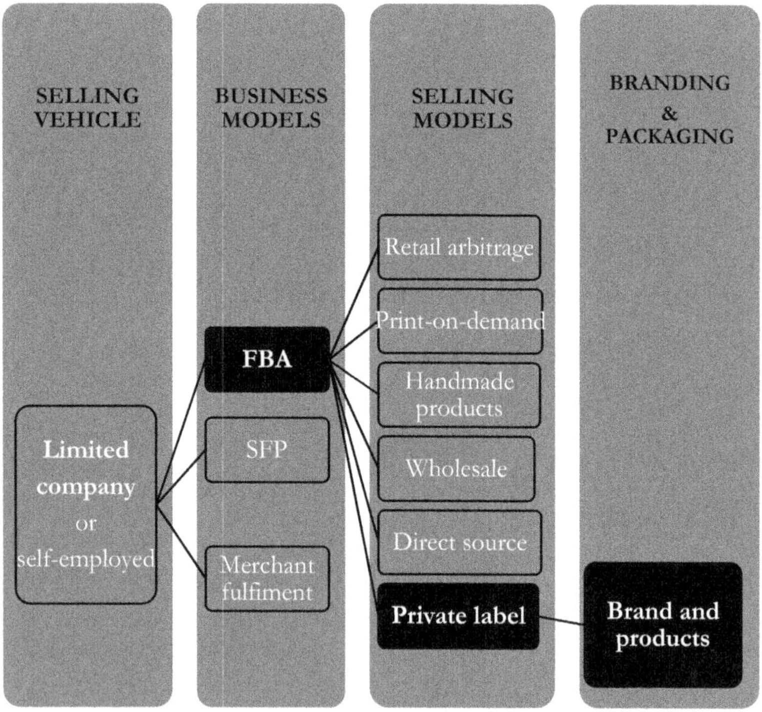

Limited Companies—these are either "limited by shares" or "limited by guarantee".

Limited by Shares

These are companies created with the intention of making profits and they: (1) are legally separate from the people who run them, (2) have separate finances from their shareholders, (3) have shares and shareholders and (4) can keep any profits they make after paying taxes. These profits can be distributed to the shareholders.

Limited by Guarantee

These companies are usually "not for profit" and they: (1) are legally separate from the people who run them, (2) have separate finances from personal ones, (3) have guarantors and a "guaranteed amount"; and (4) they invest the profits they make back into themselves.

It's a no-brainer; the plan is to sell on Amazon for profit. Therefore, it would make sense that your startup is a company limited by shares.

Setting up a limited company—you can choose to set up your limited company yourself using HMRC's guide—Google "hmrc limited company guide". Using a third party will cost you between £20 and £50—at the time of print. I recommend using a third party to save time—for example, I have used a company called Simple Formations (simpleformations.com) to incorporate my limited company—they are quick and efficient.

Selling through a limited company or as self-employed ("sole trader") has its advantages and disadvantages:

Advantages of operating as a limited company:

1. Tax—running your business as a limited company can enable you to legitimately pay less personal tax than the self-employed. Profits from limited companies are subject to a 25% UK Corporation tax. If you are a director and shareholder of a limited company, you can split your remuneration from the company between salary and dividends. A limited company is tax efficient, as National Insurance Contributions (NICs) are not

payable on company dividends. By contrast, they are payable on salaried income—as self-employed—all your income will be subject to NIC. The rules are always changing—so make sure that you do some research before you commit to a specific selling vehicle. The HMRC website would be a good start for your research, before engaging an accountant.

2. Distinct entity—a limited company is legally separate from its owners. Everything from the bank accounts, assets, and liabilities differs from those of the shareholders. A sole trader and their business are treated as a single entity from a tax perspective.

3. Limited liability—running your business as a limited company means you have the reassurance of "limited liability". Limited liability means you will not be personally liable for any financial losses made by your startup. Therefore, a limited company can give you added protection should things go wrong. However, company directors will lose their protection if they do not conduct business by the law. "Self-employment businesses" do not enjoy such protection from specific financial and legal claims. Self-employed persons are personally liable for the debts and liabilities of their businesses.

4. Professional—for some businesses and industries, having a limited company can provide a more professional image. There are many more laws regarding commerce and business governing corporations than there are for natural persons. Therefore, there is the perception that corporations are more likely to act with "good business conscience", and behave ethically, without cutting corners.

5. Funding—can be difficult for all types of startups. It some cases it's easier to secure business finance for limited companies. Corporations have the perceived advantage of having more controls and processes to manage business risks compared to sole traders—for lenders this can mean lower lending risks.

6. Naming—once you register your company with Companies House, your company name is protected by law. No one else can use the same name as you, nor anything deemed to be too similar. However, complete brand protection comes through registering your trademarks. Refer to the Branding and Trademarks chapter.

Companies House ("the Registrar of Companies" in some countries) is the executive agency of the British Government that maintains the register of companies and is responsible for incorporating all forms of companies in the United Kingdom

7. Shareholders—a limited company can issue various classes of shares. This means you can sell part or all of the company through share transfer. Suppose your limited company has more than one shareholder. In that case, you should have an article of association ("shareholders' agreement") in place, outlining the duties and responsibilities of shareholders and directors. It can also detail what shareholders can and cannot do with their shares. This will prove invaluable should a shareholder want to exit the business.

8. Costs—some people prefer to operate as self-employed than through a limited company, because the startup and running costs are perceived to be significantly lower.

Historically, you would pay your accountant to handle the administration of a limited company, but most of these tasks can now be done quickly and painlessly through Apps. Using an online accounting App will cut the time you spend on bookkeeping. Xero or FreeAgent can be used to submit your VAT tax returns directly to HMRC. You can use Google Search to find these service providers.

Find the right accountant—it's worth spending some time to find the right accountant for your startup. Most accountants double as business advisors, and they can provide you with valuable insight into other e-commerce businesses they have worked with. So, look for an accountant who is already working with established Amazon sellers. Because I have an accounting background, I do my own accounting and I use Xero and A2X. If I wasn't an accountant, I would search for "seller forums" in Seller Central to access the Amazon Seller Forums, then use this platform to find accountants who have been recommended by other sellers.

After you have found the right accountant, talk to them about using A2X (a2xaccounting.com). A2X is an e-commerce accounting App that "transforms" bank deposit data from Amazon. It automatically categorises sales, fees, taxes and refunds and organises transactions into summaries that perfectly match the bank deposits in your accounting software. I used to find reconciling sales data vs. bank receipts and VAT returns time-consuming before I started using A2X. You and your accountant will need A2X or a similar solution to save yourselves the headaches.

9. Succession—if a shareholder wishes to retire/sell their shareholding, transferring ownership of a limited company is far easier than it would be for a non-registered business structure. If you intend to sell your business in the long run, I suggest you read the book: Built To Sell, by John Warrillow—it provides insight into the steps you can take to create a valuable sellable company. You will need to read the book so that you can step up a sellable business from day one and avoid having to modify your business three to five years down the line to make it "sellable".

I hope by now you are confident about operating as a limited company and are ready to register one and get it out of the way.

Self-employment

Is there Really No Benefit to Starting as Self-employed?— the short answer is that it depends on your circumstances. For example, if you start selling while in full employment and forecast that you will be making a loss, you might be able to save some of the tax you pay from your full-time employment in the first year or two.

In the UK, HMRC provides a tool you can use to calculate the tax that you pay. Google "HMRC estimate, tax calculator".

Say you earn £100,000 as a full-time employee in the tax year 2023. The total tax to pay HRMC that year is approximately £32k. See below.

	£	
Salary	100,000	a
Tax-free allowance	(12,570)	
Taxable pay	87,430	
Less:		
Income Tax	(27,428)	
National Insurance	(4,765)	
Total tax to pay	(32,193)	b
Net pay	67,807	**a - b**

Assume in the same 2023 year, your Amazon business makes a £30k loss as follows:

	£	% of sales excluding VAT
Sales including VAT	301,000	
Less VAT	(50,167)	
Sales excluding VAT	250,833	
Cost of sales	(122,117)	(49)%
Gross profit	128,716	51%
Gross margin	**51%**	
Less:		
Amazon advertising	(120,400)	(48)%
Non-Amazon storage	(20,000)	(8)%
Courier—from UK warehouse to Amazon's fulfilment centres	(6,000)	(2)%
Accounting, tax, and consulting	(4,316)	(2)%
Other administration costs	(3,000)	(1)%
Product research, photos, promotions, samples and listings	(5,000)	(2)%
Total operating and administrative costs	(158,716)	(63)%
Profit before tax	(30,000)	(12)%
Taxation	—	
Net profit	(30,000)	(12)%
Net margin	**(12)%**	

As a full-time employee and self-employed Amazon seller, you can prepare a consolidated tax return. See analysis below.

	Full time employ-ment £		"Startup" as self-employ-ment £	Total £	
Income					
Sales (excluding VAT)			250,833	250,833	
Total income			**250,833**	**250,833**	
Less:					
Cost of sales			(122,117)	(122,117)	
Amazon advertising			(120,400)	(120,400)	
Non-Amazon storage			(20,000)	(20,000)	
Courier—from UK warehouse to Amazon's fulfilment centres			(6,000)	(6,000)	
Accounting, tax and consulting			(4,316)	(4,316)	
Other administration costs			(3,000)	(3,000)	
Product research, photos, promotions, samples and listings			(5,000)	(5,000)	
Total expenses			(280,833)	(280,833)	
Net loss			(30,000)	(30,000)	
Salary	**100,000**	a		**100,000**	a
Self-employment loss	(30,000) ◄			(30,000)	
Tax-free allowance	(12,570)			(12,570)	
Taxable pay	**57,430**		-	**57,430**	
Less:					
Income Tax	(15,428)		-	(15,428)	
National Insurance	(4,165)		-	(4,165)	
Total tax to pay	(19,593)	b	-	(19,593)	b
Net pay	**80,407**	**a - b**	-	**80,407**	**a - b**

Therefore, the tax refund that is due to you from HMRC when you submit your tax return is £13k. See calculation below.

	£	
Tax paid as a full-time employee and with your startup operating as limited company—see example above		32,193
Tax paid as a full-time employee and with your startup operating as self-employment		(19,593)
Tax saving/refund due from HMRC		**12,600**

Selling Models

Most startups and small businesses initially consider wholesale products and made-to-order manufactured goods. However, these are just two of six very different models for how you can start selling on Amazon. Equally important to you, applying the most effective selling model under your circumstances is about knowing how to spot profitable products on Amazon—refer to the Product Research chapter.

Product source	Best for
Retail arbitrage	E-commerce entrepreneurs, and for testing the Amazon sales waters
Print-on-Demand	Designers, artists, and anyone with ideas for "tees" and custom-printed goods
Handmade Products	Artisans and creatives producing their own products by hand.
Wholesale	Sellers who want variety without the manufacturing headaches
Direct source	Established sellers who want to sell branded products
Private Label	E-commerce entreprenuers who want to launch and sell products under their own brand on a limited budget

Below is a brief description of each method. The rest of the book focuses on private label. Don't worry too much about exploring these other selling models. I am telling you about them so that you are aware of what other Amazon sellers are doing—however, in my opinion, your focus should be private label.

1. Retail Arbitrage—in retail arbitrage, you purchase deeply discounted retail products and resell them on Amazon. It sounds simple, but doing it right—meaning profitably—takes some work. Retail arbitrage sellers are absolute pros when hunting for deeply discounted and clearance deal products in their local stores and then pushing them through Amazon.

2. Print-on-demand Products ("POD")—are essentially dropship items that are custom-made when a customer places an order. POD manufacturers handle everything for you, from sourcing and storing all available products to printing and shipping items as ordered.

3. Handmade Products—suitable for crafts persons or artisans selling products they make by hand. The listing rules on Amazon Handmade are stringent—more so than Etsy in many cases. Many Amazon Handmade sellers are Etsy sellers looking to expand their reach by tapping into Amazon's vast audience.

4. Wholesale—this is simply reselling goods made by other companies. This is a widespread way for startups looking to explore the profit potential of different product categories. It's easy to source products from wholesale suppliers and manufacturers online via wholesale marketplaces like Alibaba and Thomasnet. The problem with this is that you actually don't own or control the customers nor the brand, and the competition is fierce.

5. Direct Source—this is similar to wholesale, with direct sourcing. You purchase goods directly from the manufacturer. You can buy specific branded products already selling well on Amazon at lower per-unit costs than wholesale prices. You can also have branded custom, "made to order" products that stand out from the competition.

You have probably guessed this one. If I'm going to be selling products that are branded already, aren't other people going to do the same thing, and could they sell at lower prices—and if other sellers charge less than me, will I lose customers? Yes, you will, and for the same products, but with different sellers, Amazon recommends sellers with the lowest price first. So the seller with the lowest price wins the "Buy Box".

Buy Box (now called the "Featured Offer") is a widget on the top right (on your desktop), of a product listing above the "Add to Cart" and "Buy Now" buttons. See the screenshot below.

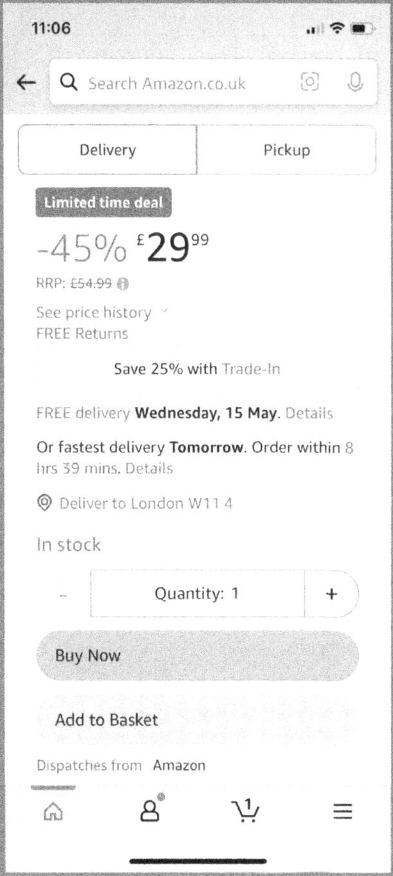

That spot shows the offer selected by Amazon as the best one and shown to buyers who can add that offer to their shopping carts with one click.

When one of your items appears this way on a product detail page, it's called the Featured Offer and it's what the Amazon algorithm considers to be the best offer in terms of price and delivery. FBA sellers are automatically eligible to win the Buy Box. FBA and SFP products are prioritised in the competition for the Buy Box.

6. Private Label—this is an offshoot of direct sourcing. It's a great way to find products to sell on Amazon under your brand. Private label manufacturers manufacture goods, then label, and tag or package them under their own brand. This is "the backbone of Chinese factories"! You can find private-label products in virtually any category, from personal care items and cosmetics to kitchen tools, pet supplies, gourmet foods, and much more.

The main disadvantage is that you still have to order private-label products in large quantities, so there are upfront costs. Moreover, labelling and other customisation factors come with added costs. With that said, the private-label model tends to top the recommended sourcing options for startups looking to build a valuable brand on and off Amazon.

It's no secret that I'm a big fan of the private-label model—you can reduce your product launch costs by doing most of the work yourself, and the model has the best exit strategy, whereby you can end up with a precious and reputable brand that you can sell after a couple of years ("....my precious").

In this book, we will focus on selling private-label products. These products will be manufactured in China. However, they can be manufactured anywhere worldwide if your numbers stack up.

5 BRANDING

Branding

Let's summarise. Here are the steps you must complete before you can design your packaging: step 1—find what you are going to sell on Amazon; step 2—decide the brand name; step 3—register the brand name; step 4—only after the brand name has been approved and registered by the IPO should you begin designing your packaging and step 5—register your brand with the Amazon Brand Registry.

The secret to a perfect brand name

"In the past, the surname of a founder would suffice. Now, brand names are more painstakingly contrived.

Here's a quiz. Take the following seven names: Emma, Simba, Leesa, Purple, Nectar, Casper and Tuft & Needle. Can you spot what they have in common? (Hint: you may need to sleep on it.)

Answer: they're all online mattress retailers. Only Tuft & Needle gives the slightest suggestion of the product. The rest could be hawking anything from single-origin espresso to electric scooters.

The earliest brand names typically followed the surnames of their founders. When an English candlemaker, William Procter, teamed up with an Irish soap maker, James Gamble, in 19th-century America, he created a brand styling that makes up in longevity what it lacks in imagination. Today's brand names tend to be more painstakingly contrived. The founders of Warby Parker, an online eyewear company, sifted through thousands of iterations before settling on a mashup of two characters from Jack Kerouac's

"On the Road".

Some names are reached by playing around with words. The messaging company Slack, for example, made an acronym out of "Searchable Log of All Conversation and Knowledge". The name also neatly conjures up the productivity problems its technology is there to solve. Start-ups want short names like Slack that stand out yet are somehow familiar (psychologists call this sweet spot in human preference "optimal distinctiveness"). Many companies try to achieve this by using the first names we might give our children. Casper, an online mattress seller, was named after an old college friend of the founders. "We realised that having something that makes it feel like it could be a person actually kind of lets your guard down a little bit and lets you have that deeper connection," explained Neil Parikh, one of its founders. With nearly 200 other firms in the online mattress market, consumers might also not have noticed another company with "sleep" or "rest" in its name.

We assign meanings to the aural quality of words and their semantic associations: Casper sounds soothing, a soft echo of "whisper". One study has found that participants assumed an ice cream called "Frosh" would be smoother and creamier than one named "Frish". Casper also has the combination of familiarity and novelty that makes for a fashionable baby name.

Both parents and brand creators need to be sure that the name they give their baby passes the grocery store test—how does it sound when you call it aloud in a public place? In both cases, it should be a name they can grow into and age gracefully with. After all, brands want us to forge with them what we have with our kids: a lifelong bond"—The Economist (2020), "The Secret To A Perfect Brand Name."

Choose a name that can be used on multiple products—this will enable you to use the same brand name for additional products you launch; for example, think of the sub-brands under "Virgin" and "Apple"—like: Virgin Atlantic, Virgin Records, Virgin Trains, Virgin Money, Apple Music, Apple Watch and Apple iPhone.

You can use this strategy to launch additional products after your first product under what would be a "known brand". When Apple launched a watch for the first time—no one questioned what they knew about watchmaking, because most people were already familiar with the brand.

Trademarks

This section is going to be an easy read. By now, you have a good idea of what you will be selling, and you have a brand name in mind—so it makes sense that you register that brand name so that no one else can use it.

A trademark is a unique and recognisable word, phrase, symbol or design that represents a business or product and legally differentiates it from other products and businesses of its kind. It is a form of intellectual property—and can be a logo, slogan, brand or just the name of a product. For example, the Nike Swoosh®, McDonald's double arches, and Apple's apple with a bite taken out are examples of designs that act as trademarks. Meanwhile, slogans like Nike's "Just do it", and MacDonald's "I'm lovin' it" also act as trademarks.

A founder, manufacturer/company gives a brand name to a particular product. A brand name has two main functions: identification and verification. It differentiates a specific product from similar products and authenticates that the product is genuine, not a fake. Sometimes, a brand name can simply be the name of the founder, for example, Martha Stewart, Ford, Kellogg's, or Ralph Lauren. The word "NIKE" is a brand name, and the Nike Swoosh® is a trademark. When you register a trademark, you can register both a trademark and brand name or just the brand name.

When you register your trademark, you'll be able to: (1)—take legal action against anyone who uses your brand without your permission; (2)—put the ® symbol next to your brand name or trademark—to show that it's yours, registered with the relevant authorities and warn others against using it; and (3)—sell and license your brand.

A trademark lasts 10 years. You must renew your trademark every 10 years to keep it in force.

What you can register—your trademark can include: words, sounds, logos; colours; or a combination of any of these.

What you cannot register—your trademark cannot: (1) be offensive, for example, it can't contain swear words or pornographic images; (2) describe the goods or services it will relate to; for example, the word "cotton" cannot be a trademark for a cotton textile company; (3) be misleading; for example, using the word "organic" for goods that are not organic; (4) be too familiar or non-distinctive, for example, a statement like "we lead the way"; (5) be just a generic shape associated with your business; for example, if you sell apples, you cannot trademark the shape of an apple; (6) make use of national flags you do not have permission to use; and (7) make use of official emblems or hallmarks, for example, coats of arms.

You may not be able to register your trademark if it's similar to a trademark registered by another business that sells the same goods or services.

If you are going to be registering your trademark in the UK, refer to this two-minute video from the UK Intellectual Property Office ("IPO") for details:
https://www.youtube.com/watch?v=_CM9-4Qrj3I

How Much It Costs to Register a Trademark

Registering a trademark in the UK costs at least £170—at the time of print. It will usually cost more depending on your circumstances, for example, how many classes of goods or services you want to protect in your brand.

IP offices worldwide use a trademark classification system that groups similar goods or services into 45 classes. This is referred to as the Nice classification (NCL). Each class contains a list of terms. These cover all the goods or services included in that class—goods are in classes 1 to 34; and services are in classes 35 to 45.

All classes have a broad heading explaining what's covered in that class. This is only a general indication and does not include all the goods or services in that class. For example, a single online trademark application covering one class will cost £170. The same application covering three classes will cost £270—thus: £170 for the application and first class and £100 for the two extra classes, at £50 per class.

The Application Process

You must send details of your trademark and the goods you want to use your trademark on to the IPO. You can send your application online or by post. Applying online is quicker. The IPO will check that your trademark is not the same as or similar to any existing trademarks and publish details of your application in the journal—in case anybody wants to oppose it.

If there are any issues with your application, the IPO will let you know by post, and you will have to resolve them before you can register your trademark. If there are no issues, it usually takes three to four months from the date of application for the IPO to grant your trademark.

Plan ahead—when registering your trademark, include as many classes as possible. For example, if you apply to register your trademark for clothing in class 25: clothing, footwear, and headgear. A year later, you decide to expand your brand into handbags. Since the application you have filed only covers clothing—class 25, you must file another application to register your trademark in class 18—which covers handbags. The extra cost of the new application can be avoided by including both classes in the first application. You'd also avoid paying two sets of renewal fees in 10 years.

Below is a timeline of the application process in the UK.

1—Before you apply

Decide the classes to register in

Check if anyone has already registered your trademark

2—Prepare your application

Have details of slogans, illustrations or terms you want to register ready

3—Payments

Online applications cost £170 and £50 for each additional class

4—After you apply

The IPO will:

Examine your application within 2 weeks;

Search for similar trademarks; and

Publish your trademark in the trademarks journals for 2 months—if there is no opposition—register it 2 weeks later

5—Opposition

If it is opposed, you withdraw the application; or

Defend your application—you will pay legal costs

6—When your trademark is registered

The IPO will send you a certificate to confirm registration

You can sell, licence, market and mortage your trademark

Register Your Trademark Overseas—registering a trademark in the UK only protects your brand in the UK and the Isle of Man. As your business grows, you must register your trademark in other countries.

Do your research. Ensure that the trademark you want to register is not already in use—don't make the mistake I made. I registered a trademark for "Nordic O2"—designed the packaging before the IPO office approved it. A couple of weeks later, I received a 200-page document from O2—Telefonica's lawyers, the mobile phone network, advising me that I couldn't use the trademark because "Nordic O2" could be confused with O2's brand in the Nordic region. I asked the O2 lawyers if they could refund me for the costs I incurred and not fight their opposition. My expenses were peanuts to them, so they quickly agreed.

Once you have selected a brand name, search for it on Google, Facebook, Instagram, YouTube etc., to ensure no one is using it.

Amazon Brand Registry ("ABR")

ABR is a program designed for brand owners and manufacturers selling on Amazon—it enables them to register their brand and access a series of tools to protect and enhance it. Before enrolling your brand in ABR, you must register your trademark/brand with the IPO.

"Amazon Brand Registry helps you protect your intellectual property and create an accurate and trusted experience for customers on Amazon. Available for brand owners, manufacturers and vendors worldwide, over 700k brands, are already registered, and this number is expected to rocket alongside the number of sellers on the marketplace" —2021 Amazon Brand Protection Report

ABR Eligibility Requirements

To be eligible for ABR, your brand must have an active registered trademark in each country you wish to enrol in, or have a pending trademark application filed via Amazon IP Accelerator.

Pending registration means that you have submitted a trademark application to the IPO—and are waiting for the IPO's approval confirmation. The trademark owner must submit ABR applications.

To enrol your brand with ABR, Google—"amazon brand registry" and then sign into Seller Central ("SC") using your usual SC password. From the main menu, select "Stores", followed by "Manage Stores" and then follow the onscreen instructions. You will need to provide the following information as part of the enrolment process: (1) the trademark registration number—the IPO provides this, (2) a list of product categories in which your brand should be listed, and (3) the brand name—the trademark for your brand must appear on your products/packaging, and you could be asked to provide images that depict this—so make sure to take photos of your branded product and packing from the samples you have received from your manufacturer.

After submitting this information, Amazon will verify that you are the trademark's rights owner by sending you a verification code to complete the enrolment process. After this, you will get access to the full ABR suite of benefits and features that will help protect your Brand.

ABR features and benefits include: (1) automated protections—stopping bad listings before publication. Amazon implements predictive protections using advanced machine learning to prevent bad listings; (2) report a violation—you will be able to search Amazon's catalogue to easily look for: potential trademark, copyright, patent and design rights violations (if you find an infringement, you can report it through Seller Support) and (3) brand Registry support—a dedicated team to support you with brand registry-related issues.

6 PACKAGING

"If you order something from Selfridges the inside of the box is actually yellow on a shiny backdrop and with a Selfridges logo, and a bit of tissue paper. Packing is when a product first becomes a brand"—Roy Sutherland, YouTube interview, "The Diary Of A CEO"

Now that your brand name has been approved and registered with the IPO, you must design the product packaging. Your packing designs should appeal to your target market. There are various third parties you can use for this service. If you have time, you can design your packaging using software such as Adobe Illustrator. If you have the stamina, you can sign up for a free Adobe Illustrator trial and complete your packaging design within the free trial period. Google search "Adobe Illustrator Free Trial".

If you don't have a design background, this will be time-consuming—believe me, I have tried and didn't get very far! You can access Adobe Illustrator through a monthly subscription of less than £30 at the time of print. Designers on platforms such as Fiverr (www.fiverr.com), 99designs (www.99designs.co.uk) and Upwork (www.upwork.com) can help you design your packaging within a week.

Fiverr—this popular website connects you to freelancers from around the globe, offering many services. Search the site for "product packaging design", and you will receive thousands of results with a wide range of prices, from as little as £10 to a few hundred pounds. Regarding getting professional packaging designs, you will probably find the most cost-effective option here. From my experience, a drawback of freelancers on Fiverr is that you must have a concrete design idea. The designers here tend not to do well with vague ideas and won't go above and beyond to create an original design for you. Plenty of competent designers are on the website, but generally, they do only what they are told.

To circumvent this problem, be sure to do your research. Find elements in existing product designs that you'd like to incorporate within your own and present these to your designer. Stay firm; the first delivery your designer returns to you with might fall short of your expectations. This is OK. Don't be afraid to express your concerns; have the patience to work through several revisions. A small investment of time and patience will engender substantial dividends in the long run.

Upwork and 99designs—moving up in quality and, of course, price are Upwork and 99designs. They are websites that allow you to post jobs and have freelancers come to you with proposals and bids. You interview them, hire the best fit, and, depending on the agreed-upon details of the invoice, pay a fixed fee or an hourly rate. Remember that you will pay somewhere in the ballpark of £150 to £800. Consider whether a packaging design of this calibre is appropriate for your product. For certain products, this is unnecessary, meaning you can have a cheaper, simpler design and still sell many units on Amazon.

I recommend Fiverr. You can have good quality designs from Fiverr freelancers if you define your targeted audiences and provide them with pictures of similar products that are doing well on Amazon.

Review your samples from the manufacturer in their intended packaging—after your packaging designs are complete, send the print files to the manufacturer so they can send you your product samples in their intended packaging. In the world of commercial printing, each print run usually has a minimum print quantity. Don't be surprised if your manufacturers tell you that for your samples—only 2/3 units, they will charge you for printing, say, 500 units—it's just how it works with some commercial printers. Therefore, ask them to print the 500 packaging units and keep the rest for later when you place a bulk order. Depending on your packaging or designs, expect to pay about US$0.50 per unit—at the time of print—for a two-litre box. Your manufacturer will manage this for you and they will liaise directly with the printers

When designing your packaging, remember to add your product bar code and contact details on the package so that customers can contact you if needed.

Design Beautiful Product Packaging to Boost Loyalty

Product packaging is designing, evaluating, and producing a container for your products.

For e-commerce businesses, shipping and fulfilment represent the most direct touch point and connection with a customer. It is also one of the most underused marketing opportunities. Packaging came out of a need to protect products during the shipping process, but focusing solely on function means you might need to look into the potential marketing impact of your packaging. Done well, the proper packaging and unboxing experience is a chance to deliver a functional product and create a memorable moment for your customers.

Many online retailers create a branded product packaging experience to delight customers and improve profitability—ideally, one that's both memorable and shareable.

Importance of product packaging design

Online stores have fewer touch points to deliver delight than physical retail. The advantage of the efficiency of online shopping can come at the cost of the tactile, hands-on experience with a product before making a purchase.

Packaging has become an extension of your brand for online retailers. Take Apple, for example. The brand is known for high-end, glossy, and refined products, just like the package it's shipping. While not all entrepreneurs have "Apple's kind of budget", you can incorporate different, less costly ways to delight customers at every journey stage.

Fundamentally, people like sharing great experiences they've had. Search for "unboxing" on Google, and you'll find countless blog posts, images, and videos. Many of those pieces of content were created by customers, further helping a brand launch and get its name out to more people. Building a long-term, growing brand means bringing customers back repeatedly. Repeat customers will spend more with your business, and investing in retention and customer loyalty can move you off the acquisition treadmill where you're always trying to find new customers.

Custom product packaging

Custom packaging is a great way to create a unique unboxing experience and show customers what you value. Plus, you can print all over your packaging to present your brand in new ways and create a satisfying customer experience.

How to create a custom packaging experience

Many elements must work together when creating a well-designed branded packaging and unboxing experience, but you don't have to include every available option.

Instead, decide which packaging solutions deliver the best experience and most value for your customers. Strategically investing in some of these solutions can go a long way in creating an unboxing experience your customers won't soon forget.

(1) Promotional material or a business card—business cards offer a cost-effective way of adding small promo pieces to your package. Remember, they don't have to mimic the aesthetics of corporate business cards. This printed content serves as reading material that deepens the brand's relationship with customers. You can also include a personal note or special instructions to help customers get more value out of your product—the possibilities are endless and relatively inexpensive.

(2) Custom note—though handwritten notes may be tricky to scale, startups are fighting to earn every customer. Connecting with shoppers through a personal, genuine note or card can make all the difference—handwritten messages (or anything close) show customers you care and that real people are powering your brand.
(3) Manuals and Educational Materials—if you sell products that need a little "how-to," add instructions inside your packaging. You want to ensure your customers understand how to use the product.
(4) Sample or gift—with time, depending on the products that you sell, consider including a free sample of another product. Ideally, you'll choose something your shopper will likely be interested in. For example, if they purchased shampoo, throw in a small sample of complementary conditioner. This tactic can help you cross-sell by introducing a customer to new products"— Shopify.com (2023) "Design Beautiful Product Packaging To Boost Loyalty"

You can use this tactic down the line when adding complementary products to your brand. Ensure you run your numbers correctly, as any other samples you add to your original packing will increase their weight, size, and, consequently, the FBA fees.

Creating a memorable unboxing experience can be your business's competitive edge to generate repeat purchases and attract new customers.

"At the end of the day, you're not building an e-commerce company, you're building a brand that has e-commerce as its core distribution channel."—Andy Dunn, Founder—Bonobos

In my product manuals, I provide customers with details of my website. When they contact me via the website, I automatically obtain their email addresses, as they would have provided that information in the contact form. You can use the email addresses to offer discounts and promote new products. Ensure that you give customers the option to allow you to contact them in the future when they are completing the contact form and in future, the option to unsubscribe—obviously.

Think of multi-use packaging—the best packaging is something that consumers can use for something else. For example, many food products come with packaging that can be used for storage purposes. This adds value to the customer and your brand, as customers are likely to remember your brand when shopping, especially if they are using your packaging regularly.

Source: Pinterest

Packaging should be viewed as something other than a cardboard box, bottle, bag, etc., in which your product is transported. Use it to let your character and creativity come out and help get people hooked on what you are selling.

7 SOURCING

Simply put, sourcing refers to finding products from third parties to resell on Amazon. The third parties include manufacturers, distributors, wholesalers, and drop-shipping agents.

Sourcing from China

For your private-label startup, you can use domestic or overseas manufacturers. Anything produced locally has apparent merits. You don't have to worry about the language barriers. You can easily visit the vendor/manufacturer and see what they are doing—and who doesn't like flaunting "Made in the UK", "Made in Germany" etc., on their product? It's a home run! That said, domestic manufacturing can be costly—and for that reason, we will focus on sourcing from China.

Why China? (1) China employs the most significant manufacturing labour force in the world; (2) a wide selection of products; (3) lower production costs due to an abundance of labour and competition among manufacturers; (4) quick turn-around time; and (5) China ships to every corner of the globe.

You can find reliable manufacturers through Alibaba.com (www.alibaba.com) and Global Sources (www.globalsources.com). Working with a freight forwarder, the manufacturer can help you ship your products directly from their factory to Amazon warehouses while sitting at home. All praise to the power of the internet.

Alibaba is a global B2B e-commerce platform connecting e-commerce sellers with millions of product manufacturers. This is where you can go to create custom products for your brand. Whether you are the buyer of a large corporation/a startup operating from a garage, you can sign up and source products from Alibaba. The quality of manufacturers that you will find on Alibaba is excellent. As you continue your research, you will see that those same manufacturers work with some of the world's biggest brands, such as Tesco, Sainsbury's, Target, Walmart, Home Depot and B&Q.

Many Amazon sellers use Alibaba because of its user-friendly App and low prices. Most manufacturers that you will come across on the platform are based in China. Any seller can go to Alibaba right now and search for the type of products they're interested in, and the search results will yield hundreds of potential manufacturers. Finding a manufacturer for your products has never been easier. However, some work needs to be done to weed out manufacturers who are not a "good fit"—we will cover this issue in the following pages. As a private-label seller with a unique brand, Alibaba is an excellent venue for finding manufacturers who can turn your product ideas into a reality. It's worth noting that your product doesn't have to be unique for it to sell well on Amazon. Your brand is what needs to stand out. You can launch similar products under a different brand and still secure a market share. While it's a challenging task, it's possible to establish a profitable business using this model.

Do not use Alibaba to purchase branded products—while there are many reputable manufacturers, known as "verified suppliers" on Alibaba some might try to sell counterfeit products, products that look too similar or resemble big brands such as Adidas, Nike, and Phillips etc. Some products could look tempting to sell, but you should refrain from pursuing them. Selling counterfeit goods on Amazon is strictly prohibited; you'll be banned permanently from selling there if you ignore their anti-counterfeiting policy.

Is Alibaba safe—in short—yes! But there are things you need to look out for when selecting manufacturers, for example, how long they have been in business and whether they are "verified". You must contact multiple manufacturers and order samples to evaluate before placing a bulk order.

Alibaba offers a secure payment portal for all transactions, so you can be assured that your payment or credit card information is safe. Alibaba also provides an order protection service called Trade Assurance (www.tradeassurance.alibaba.com—"trade assurance"), which will get you your money back if the product quality is different from what you and your manufacturer agreed, and some compensation if there are delays caused by the manufacturer.

Always use the Alibaba messaging channels—ensure that all your messages, discussions and communication with the manufacturer are through the Alibaba App/website ("platforms"). If things go wrong, Alibaba will disregard any information not on their platforms.

How to Pick the Right Manufacturers on Alibaba

To get started, download the Alibaba App and register an account. You also have the option to sign up using the details of your Gmail/Google account, if you have one. Alibaba works the same way as Amazon. Use keywords to find the products you need.

Let's review an example of a product's search results from the Alibaba App. Assume that you want to sell readymade blackout curtains on Amazon. At the time of print, a search for: "blackout curtains" had the results below:

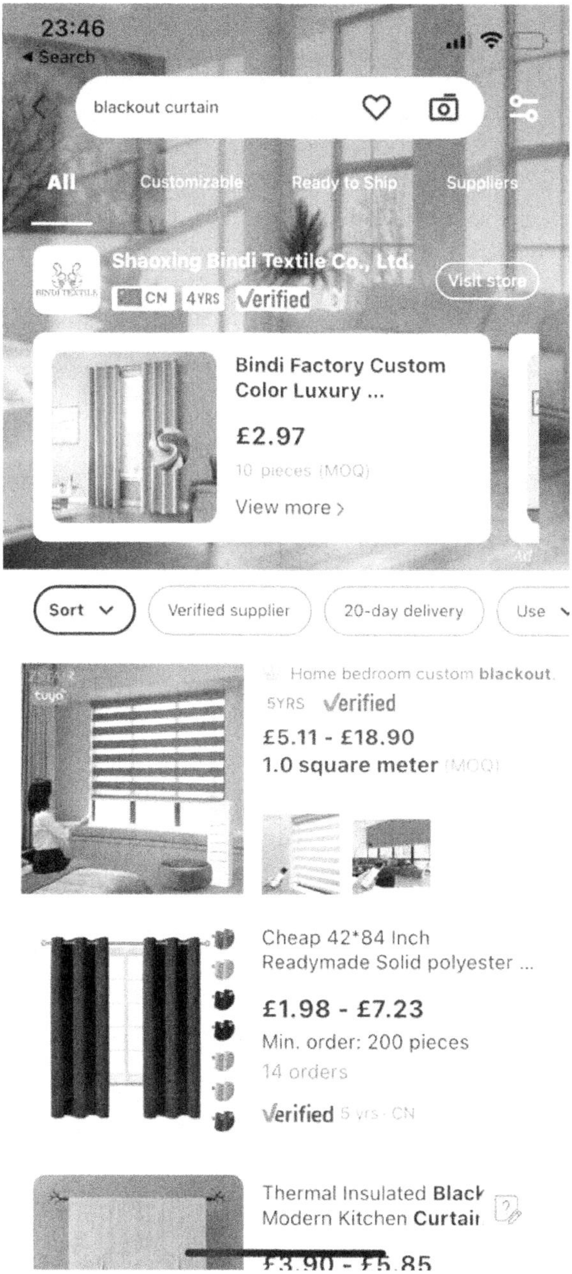
23:46
Search
blackout curtain
All
Customizable
Ready to Ship
Suppliers
Shaoxing Bindi Textile Co., Ltd.
CN
4YRS
Verified
Visit store
Bindi Factory Custom
Color Luxury ...
£2.97
10 pieces (MOQ)
View more >
Sort
Verified supplier
20-day delivery
Use
Home bedroom custom blackout
5YRS
Verified
£5.11 - £18.90
1.0 square meter (MOQ)
Cheap 42*84 Inch
Readymade Solid polyester ...
£1.98 - £7.23
Min. order: 200 pieces
14 orders
Verified 5 yrs · CN
Thermal Insulated Black
Modern Kitchen Curtai

Scroll down and see which products pique your interest. You can use these filters to specify your results: (1) supplier type; (2) product type; (3) price; (4) supplier country, and (4) certifications.

A common misconception about Alibaba is that the manufacturers are only from China. The "Supplier Country/Region" filter lets you choose a country to manufacture from. I prefer using verified manufacturers from China, as Alibaba will have performed onsite inspections for manufacturers who have their factories there.

The most important of all the filters available is "Supplier Types." Use this filer to select: "Trade Assurance" and "Verified Supplier".

After checking off these two filters, the search results will change. Go through the results and keep track of the products that look interesting. You will also see pricing information—use that only as a guide. The final price per unit will depend on the product specifications and number of units purchased—in your bulk order.

Analysing Manufacturers

Let's look at a specific listing for one of the manufacturers for "blackout curtains." Once on the listing, you can find more information about the product and the manufacturer, for example, the screenshot below:

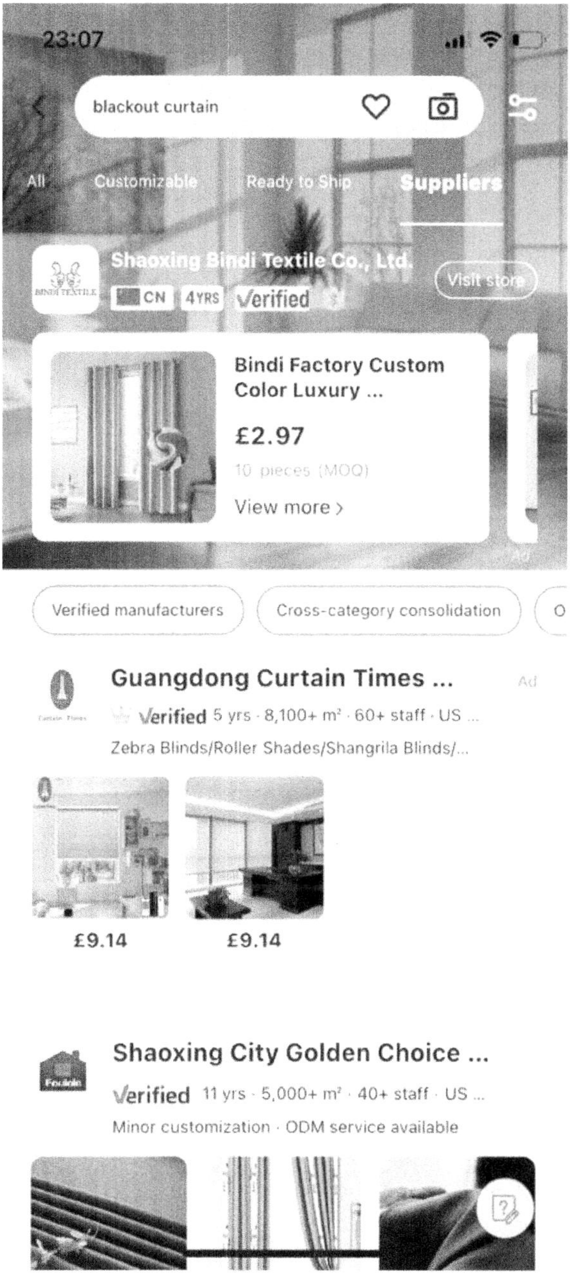
23:07
blackout curtain
All
Customizable
Ready to Ship
Suppliers
Shaoxing Bindi Textile Co., Ltd.
CN
4YRS
Verified
Visit store
Bindi Factory Custom Color Luxury ...
£2.97
10 pieces (MOQ)
View more
Ad
Verified manufacturers
Cross-category consolidation
Guangdong Curtain Times ...
Ad
Verified 5 yrs · 8,100+ m² · 60+ staff · US ...
Zebra Blinds/Roller Shades/Shangrila Blinds/...
£9.14
£9.14
Shaoxing City Golden Choice ...
Verified 11 yrs · 5,000+ m² · 40+ staff · US ...
Minor customization · ODM service available

At the top or bottom of the page, you will see the "Profile" section. This is where you can learn more about the manufacturer. Things like the annual sales; number of employees; factory size; quality control; and production capabilities. For example, see the screenshots below:

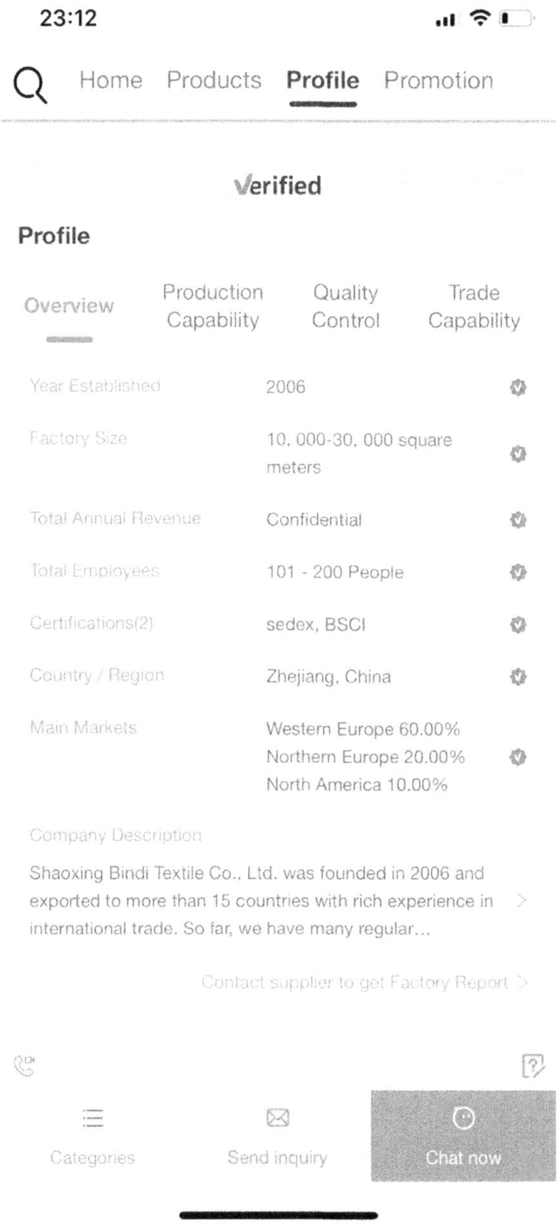
23:12
Home
Products
Profile
Promotion
Verified
Profile
Overview
Production Capability
Quality Control
Trade Capability
Year Established
2006
Factory Size
10, 000-30, 000 square meters
Total Annual Revenue
Confidential
Total Employees
101 - 200 People
Certifications(2)
sedex, BSCI
Country / Region
Zhejiang, China
Main Markets
Western Europe 60.00%
Northern Europe 20.00%
North America 10.00%
Company Description
Shaoxing Bindi Textile Co., Ltd. was founded in 2006 and exported to more than 15 countries with rich experience in international trade. So far, we have many regular...
Contact supplier to get Factory Report
Categories
Send inquiry
Chat now

Choosing Manufacturers

Contact at least 5-10 manufacturers before choosing the right one. Here are vital things to consider when selecting manufacturers to contact:

(1) Manufacturer vs Trading Companies;

Factory direct—deal with the factory directly, instead of a trading company. Trading companies are common in China; they are the middleman/the sales agent between you and the manufacturer. They usually charge a margin. Therefore, you end up paying a lot more than you should. Don't confuse a salesperson who works in the manufacturer's sales department with a separate trading company. Expect to deal with a salesperson or an account manager employed directly by the manufacturer or factory.

(2) Manufacturers who Pass the Common Thread Test;

Ensure product fit, or common thread, i.e., manufacturers who manufacture towels and only related products. Avoid a manufacturer who claims they are a towel factory but also manufacture electric toasters—completely unrelated products.

Complete a common thread check—on the Alibaba App, on a manufacturer's page, click on "More products from this supplier". Review the products you see to confirm that they are related. The screenshot below is an example of the search results for a "blackout curtains" manufacturer that I selected—and all the products shown are curtains, confirming that this manufacturer specialises in producing curtains.

01:35
◂ Search
courtans
Overview
Details
Recommended
More products from this supplier
Blackout drapery with shee...
Sample available
£3.34 - £5.01
1 meter (MOQ)
Hot sale White Sheers fold ...
One-Stop Service
£8.35 - £12.52
1 meter (MOQ)
Classic home fabric curtain...
One-Stop Service
£8.35 - £11.68
1 square meter (MOQ)
Fancy Hotel Curtain / ...
One-Stop Service
£8.35 - £12.52
1 meter (MOQ)

Alibaba has "Verified" and "Gold" suppliers. I have only used verified suppliers.

"To qualify as a Verified Supplier, a supplier's company profile, production capabilities, products and process controls have to be inspected, assessed and verified by independent third-party institutions to assure reputable and consistent expertise on Alibaba.com"—Alibaba.com

The table below shows the difference between a Gold Supplier versus a Verified Supplied—the things which Alibaba checked about a supplier/manufacturer.

	Gold supplier	Verified supplier
Basic profile		
Business license & Ownership status	☑	☑
Contact information	☑	☑
Company/Factory location	☑	☑
Company overview		
Business type and company structure (e.g. trading company, manufacturer, or both)	—	☑
Inspection videos & 360-degree VR panoramas	—	☑
Competitive advantage (e.g. low MOQ, large contract case etc.	—	☑
Trading capabilities		
Export market and market distribution	—	☑
Main clients	—	☑
R&D capabilities		
R&D staff	—	☑
Design process and devices	—	☑
Production capabilities		
Production capacity and flow	—	☑
Production machinery	—	☑
Subcontractors	—	☑
Quality control capabilities		
Quality management system and QC processes	—	☑
Product certification	—	☑
Testing capabilities	—	☑
After-sales service capabilities		
Provision of after-sales services	—	☑
Overseas after-sales services	—	☑

(3) Manufacturers who have the Right Qualifications and Experience;

Invest time in finding your soul mate—remember, finding the right manufacturer is like online dating. First, cast a wide net and narrow your choices down to 20%. Go on a few dates (keep talking to a few manufacturers and keep an open mind) to determine who is a perfect fit.

Unlike online dating, some people are attracted to people who have not been doing it for a long time. In finding a manufacturer you want, one who has been doing it with other people for a very long time! Choose manufacturers who have experience in producing for Amazon sellers. They will be familiar with Amazon's packaging and shipments labelling requirements. Alibaba will also show how many years manufacturers have been making and selling similar products.

(4) Offers Competitive Prices;

What about pricing—when sending the RFQs, you do not need to focus on pricing too much, but you should have a target price in mind. At that point, your focus must be quality and manufacturer fit. Usually, for the first and second orders, the price you will pay the manufacturer will be higher as your minimum order quantity ("MOQ") is low, and you might not make a profit; however, think long-term. You can agree to a lower unit price with your manufacturers as your order quantities increase and after you have built trust and established a good working relationship. Remember that manufacturers are still going to expect you to pay for your invoices in time as they too have working capital to manage at their end.

I am happy to accept a higher price from the manufacturers initially, for good relations and quality products. Good quality products = good product reviews, and good reviews = higher sales volumes. Generally, the business model is like that of a supermarket, think Tesco or Walmart—low margins but high volumes. Therefore, always ask yourself, what do I need to do to increase my market share—offering competitive prices to your customers is one of the most effective ways, even though this means eating into your initial target margin.

Compare manufacturers' bulk order prices—when comparing different manufacturers, use prices that the manufacturers will charge you for bulk orders and not for samples. Bulk order prices are the prices that you will pay in the long run.

(5) Returns—work with manufacturers willing to take back returns and continuously improve the quality of the products.
(6) Quality and country test—for example manufacturers with experience in selling to European and North American markets would have the relevant compliance and quality control checks in their manufacturing processes to meet the regulatory requirements for these markets.
(7) Soft Skills—select a manufacturer who demonstrates good communication and language, and is responsive and cooperative.

Contacting Multiple Manufacturers

Open the Alibaba App—on the product listing, click "Contact Supplier" to have a live chat. When you message manufacturers copies of your messages, their replies will be available to the email address linked to your Alibaba account. Here are some tips:
(1) your first communication should be detailed and precise. Use bullet points with the exact product specifications that you're looking for;
(2) you don't need a registered company to do business with Alibaba manufacturers, but you must provide some information about yourself. Manufacturers will use this information to quickly learn about you, which helps them gauge how committed you are to making a purchase;
(3) include questions about crucial specifics such as: (a) if they are a manufacturer or a trading company; (b) the minimum order quantity; (c) the cost per unit for a bulk order—this will be based on your projected annual demand. For example, 6,700 units from the "working example" in the FBA chapter; (d) sample costs—the cost of making three to four units plus airfreight to the UK; (e) lead times—for samples and bulk orders; (f) if they can add your logo to the product—you should attach your logo design files to the email or the messaging section of the App;
(4) well-established manufacturers who sell to Western markets will have in-house English-speaking sales representatives. However, English may not be their first language, so make sure that your communication is clear and straightforward; and
(5) vet each manufacturer based on the response time and how they communicate with you. If you cannot get all the answers you need from one, you can cross them off your list.

Mitigating Sourcing Risks

Purchasing your products through Alibaba is safe and secure. However, like any online marketplace, there are ways you can get scammed. Therefore, make sure you (1) purchase only from verified suppliers; (2) use trade assurance; (3) beware of counterfeit products on Alibaba. If you come across a branded product, there is a 100% chance that it is bogus; and (4) evaluate samples before placing a bulk order.

Always take advantage of Alibaba's trade assurance—when I started, I only communicated with manufacturers through Alibaba. Now that I have established relationships with them, I go to them directly when placing my orders. However, I still ask them to raise their invoices through Alibaba's Trade Assurance.

Placing an Order

Now that you have evaluated a few samples, selected the manufacturer you want to work with and are ready to place your first order, you need to be clear with your manufacturer about how many units you are ordering. The manufacturer will then prepare the following documentation for you: (1) pro-forma invoice; (2) commercial invoice—you can get this later in the procurement process; your freight forwarder will need it when processing your products through customs; (3) picking list—your freight forwarder will need it before loading your products onto the ship, and (4) trade assurance agreement ("TAA")— this is a standard contract provided by Alibaba between you and the manufacturer. If there are specific things that you would like to agree with the manufacturer, ensure that they are included in the agreement before you sign it. You can add documents and images ("attachments") as appendices to the TAA.

For the avoidance of doubt—you can ask the manufacturer to include pictures of the final sample in the trade assurance agreement, referencing that all units in the bulk order must be the same as the approved sample. Review these documents in detail, ensuring the number of units and the cost per unit are correct. Remember to recalculate the totals. I once paid an incorrect amount to a manufacturer. Luckily, it was lower than the amount I was meant to pay, and I had to top up the manufacturer before they could issue a Bill of Lading. To avoid delays later in the process, ensure that all the documents have the correct amounts.

Also, ensure that your contact details in the documents are accurate, for example, the billing, postal, and delivery addresses, especially if they are different. You want to avoid having shipping containers with your products delivered to your home! Especially the Bill of Lading—make sure you have double-checked it. It's almost impossible to change it once it's been issued. You need a court order to change a Bill of Lading in China!

Use the best available exchange rates. Through Alibaba's trade assurance, you can pay the manufacturer through bank transfer, credit card, and other options. Keep an eye on the exchange rates applied to each payment method, as they can vary significantly. I prefer paying using my American Express credit card and rack-up those air miles; however, Alibaba caps the amount you can pay with a credit card at a USD $15k per single transaction—at the time of print, and manufacturers do not like to split invoices into separate USD $15k tranches

Offline supplier research

Trade Fairs or Exhibitions

The most popular Chinese trade fair is the Canton Fair (www.cantonfair.org.cn/en-US). Due to Covid, it can now be accessed online.

8 SHIPPING

In this chapter, we will look at getting your products from your manufacturer in China into an Amazon FC in the UK/the country where your Amazon marketplace is based. Novice sellers can go through their manufacturers to arrange their first shipment, since it will be small.

However, do your research and compare prices. I have had a manufacturer quoting a higher shipment price than DHL. The beauty of using DHL, in the UK is that you pay in 30 days—subject to DHL's credit approval—after your products have arrived at a UK port of entry. This means that you might be able to sell some of your products before your shipping invoice and import duty are due.

Most manufacturers on Alibaba have worked with Amazon sellers and can help you get your products into a FC with ease. If the manufacturer agrees to arrange the shipping on your behalf, their invoice will include manufacturing and shipping costs. If your shipment is over 200 kg or 440 lbs, you will most likely benefit from using a freight forwarder ("forwarder"), as they offer competitive prices for larger and heavier cargo.

A forwarder is a third party who provides a shipping service, communicates with your manufacturer, and coordinates your shipping. They will know what to do each step of the way, including handling the paperwork that is needed to clear your products through customs. A forwarder can give you a quote after you have told them the details of your cargo, including its weight and dimensions.

The diagram below shows the most cost-effective mode of transportation to use based on shipment weight:

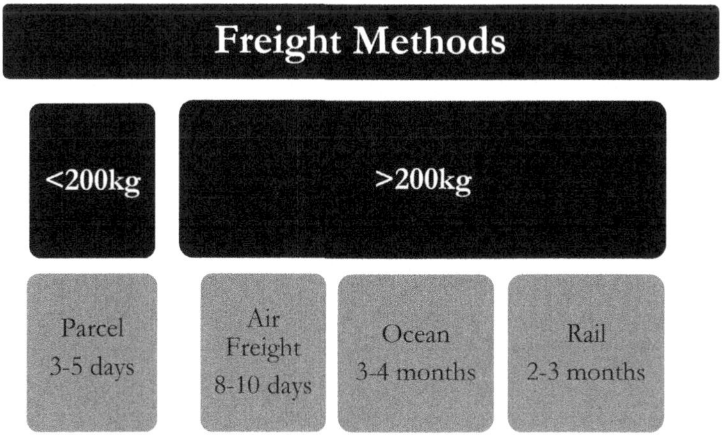

You can use rail when importing from China into mainland Europe and the United Kingdom. I bet you didn't know that there was a train from China to the UK, did you?

The size of your shipment will determine whether it's boxed, palletised, or shipped in a container, full or partial—less than container load ("LCL"). For bulk shipments, I always prefer a forwarder such as DHL/Regional Express, as they have a UK office I can call when I get nervous that things are taking too long. Regional Express are a UK-based forwarder (www.regionalexpress.co.uk).

Get quotes online for small shipments—for small air parcels, DHL, UPS, and FedEx can give you a quote online if you have the dimensions and weight of your shipment. UPS and DHL are my go-to suppliers for small parcels.

Below is a list of things you will need to know before completing your first international shipment:

(1) Incoterms—are standard freight terms used in international shipping agreements. Simply put, they describe who is responsible and liable for moving your products from point A to point B. Most manufacturers will have a preferred incoterm and you should agree with them on the methods you will use before you sign the Alibaba Trade Assurance. It will affect the total cost you pay them directly for that order. There are 11 different types, and the most common are:

FOB (Free on Board)—means the manufacturer is responsible for getting your goods from their factory to the port. This cost is added to the manufacturing cost.

EXW (Ex Works)—you are responsible and liable for the entire shipment from door to door. This is when you would usually need a forwarder to step in.

I prefer Ex Works—in instances where I have used the manufacturer to arrange the cargo for me, it caused so much confusion, and I sometimes ended up paying a lot more. At one point I had a shipping container go missing; the manufacturer believed it was offloaded in Germany but then it popped back onto the radar three months later after the manufacturer had fully refunded me.

With Ex Works, the manufacturer tells me when my goods have been packed and are ready for collection. The manufacturer will also advise of the dimensions, weight, number of units and cost of manufacturing. I will email this information to DHL or Regional Express asking for a quote—I usually go with the cheaper of the two. In my email, I will also copy in my contact from the manufacturer's side and ask both the manufacturer and my DHL/Regional Express contacts to copy me on all the emails. From then on, I'll sit back and watch the magic happen.

You should ask your forwarder and manufacturer any questions you have, so that you can start building your "international shipping" knowledge.

DDP (Delivered Duty Paid)—the manufacturer is responsible for arranging carriage and delivering your products to your delivery address. The manufacturer will also process your shipment through customs and pay the relevant customs duties and import taxes on your behalf —and you will have to pay the manufacturer for all the relevant costs.

FCA (Free to Carrier)—you are responsible and liable once the shipment is handed over to the carrier, typically near the port in the country of origin. As you would expect, any costs incurred by the manufacturer to get your goods to a point where they are handed over to the carrier will be recovered from you.

(2) Do You Have to Pay Customs on Alibaba—no, customs duty is paid to the Customs Office—in the UK, it's the HRMC—to whom you pay customs duty and import VAT. The VAT is refunded to you by HMRC if you are VAT-registered, after you have completed your VAT return.

(3) Do I Need an Import License to Order Shipments from Alibaba—if your manufacturer or forwarder oversees the shipment process, you don't need an import license to ship from China.

FBA Shipping Checklist—How to Create a Shipping Plan

Shipping to a FC can be confusing for new sellers. The good news is that there is a short checklist and a few decisions to make along the way. Your forwarder will handle the complex logistics and paperwork.

Plan for the busy shipping and selling periods of the year—October to December is the busiest. I always add a month to any delivery dates that manufacturers or freight forwarders promise. Occasionally, you have to chase them. For instance, sometimes a shipment may have arrived at its port of destination—but with no one processing the paperwork to get it delivered to a FC or own warehouse.

Create a shipping plan in Seller Central ("SC")

Creating a "Shipping Plan" in SC tells Amazon how many units of your products you will be sending and when, so that your shipment is not refused when it arrives at their FC. Before you can pull this off for the first time, you are going to need the following:

(1) the full name, address, phone number and email address of your manufacturer or the person who can be contacted in case anything goes wrong with the shipment;

(2) the number of units you are sending;

(3) the number of cases ("cartons") you are sending—including details of how many individual units are packed in a carton;

(4) the weight of each carton; and

(5) the size of each carton (cm x cm x cm).

To get started, log into SC and follow these steps:

(1) click "Inventory" from the main menu, followed by "Manage FBA Inventory";

(2) look for the product that you want to send to Amazon, scroll to the right and click on "Edit", followed by "Send or

Replenish.";
(3) click on "Create a New Shipping Plan", and then "Send Inventory.";
(4) enter your shipping address;
(5) if you are sending more than one unit, consider the case-packed product alternatives;
(6) proceed to "Shipping plan", which opens on a new page;
(7) the unit or case number should be entered. For example, if you want ship 10 items in a single box, enter 10 as the "units per case" and 1 as the "number of cases", then click continue. From here onwards, follow the onscreen instructions to complete your shipping plan.

If you get lost/confused while working on the above, search for "seller university" in SC and go to the shipping section. Amazon has a series of videos for completing steps like these.

Things to do before you create your shipping plan in Seller Central ("SC"):

Step 1—ask your manufacturer to pack the units first—ensuring that each carton is not over 23kg. After the manufacturer has sealed the units, they should provide you with the number of packed cartons and their dimensions. Use these dimensions in your Amazon shipping plan to generate the shipping labels.

Step 2—send the supplier the shipping labels you will have generated in SC. The manufacturer must stick these labels ("barcodes") on the cartons that they have prepared.

Step 3—creating the shipping plan will generate a unique shipment ID. The shipment ID and the carton labels are crucial. They enable the Amazon Fulfilment Centre ("FC") to identify your products. Any unlabelled cartons will be turned away. When the shipment arrives at a FC, Amazon will receive your inventory into the FC using the barcodes on your cartons. Instruct the manufacturer to attach the barcodes at the top and side of the cartons, away from the seams.

Step 4—if your shipments are large enough to use the entire shipping container ask your manufacturer to add the Amazon shipment IDs to your Bill of Lading as reference numbers so that your products are easy to track and identify. The shipment ID is generated when you create a shipping plan; it's a code that starts with the letters "FBA…".

Avoid additional costs, like unplanned prep service fees—Amazon will charge you for adding product barcodes ("GS1 barcode") if you have products that are missing product barcodes—these are different barcodes to the shipping label and ID barcodes I have referred to above. To avoid these additional charges, have the manufacturer label each unit with your GS1 barcode. Refer to the Product Listing chapter for details on how you can obtain the GS1 barcode. You also need to provide this barcode to the supplier so that they can stick it onto each unit or product's packaging. For the products I sell, or have sold, I have had the barcode printed on the packaging when designing the product package. In such a case, the manufacturer does not need to stick the barcode onto each unit manually.

In other words—if you already have the product barcode on your product's packaging, you don't need the manufacturer to label each unit with the same barcode. You will need to send only the carton labels and the shipment ID to the manufacturer.

There are numerous labelling and shipping requirements. Here are the key points:

(1) each box or carton must have only one shipping ID;

(2) each box should not weigh more than 23 kg unless it contains one large, oversized item that exceeds 23 kg. Boxes weighing more than 15kg must be marked "Heavy Package"; this label must be visible from both the top and sides of each heavy-weight container. This is to ensure that the packing is handled by at least two people in the FCs;

(3) carton dimensions should not exceed 63.5cm on any side unless the dimensions of a single delivery unit exceed 63.5cm;

(4) boxes must not be bagged or covered in stretch warp;

(5) boxes must not be covered in packing tape as it makes them harder to sort before recycling, thus preventing them from being recycled;

(6) neither point-of-sale containers nor bulk boxes may be used

for delivery, and
(7) boxes must be packaged so that the contents can withstand the rigours of transportation and processing at FCs.

> Read Amazon's guidance on FBA shipping and routing requirements. You must also share them with manufacturers, and anyone responsible for packing your products. Search "Shipping and routing requirements" in SC.

SC can tell you the status or phase of your shipment based on the update you provide. Below is what each stage means:

Working—means you have not sent the shipment.

Ready to ship—means you have entered the required information in the shipping workflow, but you haven't clicked "Mark as shipped".

Shipped—your shipment will automatically change to "Shipped" if you update SC with tracking details of your shipment. Get your forwarder/manufacturer to provide the tracking details as soon as they have them.

In-transit—means the shipment has been reported by the courier directly to Amazon to be in transit to one of Amazon's FCs. This happens when you use an Amazon-partnered carrier.

Delivered—means your shipment has arrived at the FC.

Checked-In—means the shipment has been checked into a dock at one of the FCs. I don't open the champagne yet, but I have one on ice; I will have my fingers crossed that the long wait will soon be over.

Receiving—the shipment contents are being processed into inventory to be available for customers to purchase. This process can be delayed if incorrect quantities or improperly labelled items have been sent. As soon as I see that a bulk number of units have been confirmed as received, I will pop the champagne—and let the selling begin.

Closed—all the inventory in your shipment has been processed and is available for fulfilment.

As soon as your shipment is boarded on a ship, obtain the Bill of Lading number or shipment tracking number. When you update your Amazon shipment plan with your Bill of Lading and or the shipment tracking details—Amazon will include the units in transit in determining how much capacity you have left in their FCs and in calculating your Inventory Performance Index ("IPI") score. The lower your IPI score, the lower the capacity Amazon will grant you in their FCs each month. A low IPI is usually due to a low sell-through rate and maintaining low stock levels. Search "IPI score" in SC for details.

Amazon will only investigate shipment issues when they have reached the "Closed" status—avoid wasting your time by only sending your queries to Amazon when the closed stage has been confirmed.

Amazon FCs are notoriously fussy—they will refuse to accept deliveries that are not 100% correctly packaged and labelled. I use Regional Express to overcome this when shipping from a UK warehouse to a FC. Alternatively, if you want guaranteed success, use Amazon's Partnered Carrier Programme. When creating your shipping plan, you will see the option to use an Amazon-partnered carrier in the Delivery Service section.

Things to Consider

Purchase Product Insurance—the most common incoterms do not include any insurance for your shipment. It would be best to discuss this during negotiations with your supplier or freight forwarder, to protect your goods. Don't forget to include this additional cost in your margin analysis.

Third-party Warehouse—after you have tested your product on the market and sold thousands of units, it's time to scale your business. This option will become a big cost-saver, as Amazon storage fees are usually higher than those of most third parties. However, you will still need to send your inventory to FCs in batches, in line with customer demand. During peak periods, most sellers send weekly inventory batches from third-party warehouses to FCs—you need to plan ahead to pull this off, as Amazon might not give you a delivery/receiving slot in the same week you want to send your inventory.

Amazon imposes restock limits, based on your IPI score—for example, they might limit you to only storing 5,000 units for a single item in a month. If your monthly sales demand is 7,000 units, you must send in more than one monthly shipment: 5,000 units at the beginning of the month and another 2,000 units in week 2. In this case, it will be impossible to arrange for exactly 2,000 units to be delivered directly from China to Amazon UK in two weeks. This can be achieved if your inventory is already in the UK—but not without headaches.

I have used decent couriers who occasionally get some of the basics wrong—for example, sending cartons with the incorrect labels, only for Amazon to return the shipment! As if that's not enough, the inventory was returned to a third-party warehouse wet and damaged. When you have established yourself and have the market share—rent your own warehouse to control this process "hands-on".

Be mentally prepared—some of the issues you will face will be different from mine; you will need to work out the things you can control and manage them closely, while outsourcing the rest. You still need to plan, check in, and chase on progress with contractors for the things you outsource. In summary—you will not be short of problems and issues—but don't give up!

What I have done in the past is, during October, apply for more storage space in FCs for November—i.e. ask Amazon to increase my capacity limit for the month of November. Once the capacity limit for November is approved, Amazon allows you to send inventory to their FCs during October based on the November capacity limits. There is an "extra charge" for capacity granted above your capacity limit—however, if the units that took up the additional capacity are sold within the same month, i.e. in November, Amazon also grants you "credits" against the "extra charge", leaving you in a "no loss position".

9 PRODUCT LISTING

What you are allowed to sell on Amazon depends on the product and its category. Some categories are open to all sellers, and some require a professional seller account and or additional approvals. To sell branded products—protected by copyright or trademark—you must be the legal owner of the brand, or an authorised reseller. To see a complete list of all the product categories you can sell in, search for "review category requirements" in Seller Central ("SC").

To start selling on Amazon, you must create a product listing in SC. Refer to an Amazon video on how to create a product listing, or search "introducing listings on Amazon" in SC. You need the following information at hand to create a listing:
(1) a product identifier—such as GTIN, UPC, ISBN, or EAN ("barcode") or ("GS1 barcode"), a unique code to your product. You can get this from GS1 or request an exemption. Google search "gs1 uk barcodes". An annual subscription of £143, at the time of print, will enable you to generate thousands of product identification codes. You can start with a lower subscription, as you will only launch one or a few products in your first year;
(2) an SKU—which is a product ID you create to track your inventory;
(3) offer details—including price and product condition;
(4) product details—name, brand, category, description, and images; and

(5) keywords and search terms—to help buyers find your product.

When multiple sellers offer the same product, Amazon combines data from those offers onto a single product detail page. Sellers who offer the same product can contribute to the product detail page information—or request a product detail page review from Amazon if they believe the information displayed is incorrect—this won't apply to private-label sellers as their brands are unique.

The Product Detail Page

Your product detail page displays your offers to customers and has the following: .

(1) Title—200 characters max, and you must capitalise the first letter of every word. A product title is also crucial in converting visitors to your product page into sales. Refer to the SEO chapter;

(2) Images—500 x 500 or 1,000 x 1,000 pixels to increase listing quality;

(3) Variations—such as different colours, scents, or sizes;

(4) Bullet points—short, descriptive sentences highlighting key features and benefits of your products;

(5) Featured offer (or "buy box")—the featured offer on a detail page. Customers will use this to add your products to their shopping basket;

(6) Other offers—details of other offers for the same product from other sellers showing different prices and shipping options (this won't be the case for private-label sellers); and

(7) Description—keywords improve the chances that people will find your listing.

Product Images

To understand the importance of your Amazon product images, stop and imagine a world where they don't exist. No matter how well you describe or how poetic you are about your products, customers still wouldn't honestly know what to expect and would understandably be apprehensive about buying. Convincing people to purchase something they can't see for themselves is awfully difficult; this is why product photos are essential.

Clear, high-quality product images show potential customers exactly what they'll be receiving so they can purchase with confidence. Not only are your images instrumental in driving sales, but they're also a key component in improving your click-through rate, reducing returns, and curbing negative reviews.

However, it shouldn't be a surprise that specific rules will apply. Refer to the Amazon image requirements in the SEO chapter. Getting the quality of the main image right can help your listing convert to sales with ease.

Main Image Requirements

What is your product—this might seem obvious, but you would be surprised by the number of Amazon main images that do not clearly show the product.

Your main image, or hero image, is the first image that appears on your product detail page and the one shown to customers in a search. It can also appear outside Amazon, in Google's search results. Getting this one right can be a massive boost to your bottom line.

Amazon shoppers have no shortage of products to choose from, so you want your main image to stand out, looking professional and making it abundantly clear what is being offered. If the main image's quality is poor, customers will continue scrolling and will purchase from your competitors. Since the main image is so essential to the shopping experience, there are specific Amazon standards to follow.

This link: "www.amazon.co.uk/dp/B0CHXFCYCR", is an example of a product detail page and A+ Content for an iPhone 15; the images, product features or bullet points and title clearly show and describe what is being sold—and when you see the photos, you would want (or need!) one, wouldn't you?

Attracting Customers

When your products go live on Amazon, there are several things you can do to attract customers. The Amazon Flywheel describes Amazon's method for driving growth. You too can use some of the strategies that Amazon have used to grow your startup—Amazon is living proof that these strategies work and are highly effective.

I like shopping on Amazon because of the excellent customer experience—a good customer experience quickly solves the customer's problem. When I see something I want on the Amazon App at a competitive price, I order it with one click, and the next day or two it arrives at my doorstep!

The Amazon Flywheel is heavily focused on ensuring that the customer gets the best experience when shopping on Amazon. The Flywheel is a virtuous cycle that is fed by its momentum. Since Amazon's founding 40 years ago, the flywheel concept has guided the company's core principles and is the driving force behind its rapid ascent.

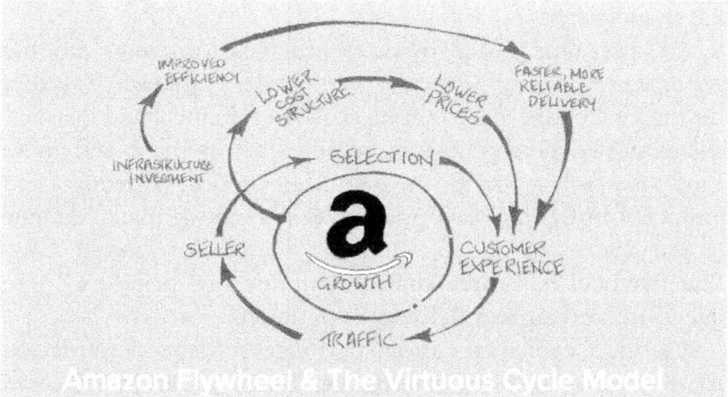

Source: Charlesleon.UK, Business Strategy

Amazon has always been focused on the customer experience; in fact, they espouse a customer obsession as one of their essential qualities. Legend has it that Jeff Bezos sketched the strategy on a napkin in 2001. Sounds familiar?—there is something similar in the movie: Knives Out 2—Daniel Craig is in it, I should mention.

Since 2001, the Flywheel has been Amazon's key marketing

strategy and business model. But the flywheel is more than just strategy/concept; it is a mindset. It speeds up growth by investing as much as possible into the customer experience because the customer experience will generate the impetus for the flywheel to spin.

Amazon was listed on the NASDAQ stock exchange in May 1997 and was loss-making for years before becoming profitable, proving that Bezos's unconventional business model had merit. By 2018, Amazon had a 43.5% share of America's online spending.

The breakthrough into profitability came when Amazon invited third-party sellers to their platform. For any other business, this would be the equivalent of inviting your competitor to sell from your own shop—ridiculous, right? By inviting other sellers in, Amazon improved the extent of its product offering, improving the customer experience and, at the same time, improving its cost structures. With third-party sellers competing against each other by lowering customer prices, the Flywheel could only become bigger and faster.

A bigger and faster flywheel provided Amazon with the resources to bring expensive processes in-house, further improving leverage and lowering costs on fulfilment and logistics. Lower fulfilment and logistics costs draw in more and more third-party sellers, who increase the product offering—and compete by offering lower prices to customers—I think you now get the idea.

The flywheel has three main elements: low prices; a huge selection; and a great delivery experience.

The more contented customers you have, the more traffic you get. So, rather than monetising the traffic, Amazon increased customer satisfaction. A significant part of Amazon's strategy is to reinvest cash generated into the business, further lower prices, and fuel programs like Amazon Prime and AWS (Amazon Web Services). The flywheel gathers momentum, with the advantages and reach also being passed on to customers, employees and third-party sellers—and then feeds from them. Initially, it takes a lot of force, in the form of capital and infrastructure, to get the flywheel spinning. As momentum is built up, it begins to rotate more efficiently, storing energy for later release.

"…you're growing the company. A side benefit of our growth over the last 10 years has been that we build a lower cost structure, so as we get bigger we get to leverage our buys, we get to leverage the fulfilment infrastructure, and logistics infrastructure, we get to leverage the website and that lowers the cost per unit of everything that we do… we have two choices we can keep that cash paid as dividend or lower our prices. As you know over the years, we've chosen to lower our prices which completes again another cycle of great customer experience." —Jeff Wilke, CEO, Amazon Worldwide Consumer

You can apply the flywheel's principles to generate momentum for the products you want to launch and lower your advertising cost of sale ("ACOS"). These are: customer experience; traffic; and pricing

The section below details how you can apply these to your startup.

(1) Customer Experience

Provide fast shipping—you will achieve this by using FBA. Customers often shop for products with the Amazon Prime badge.

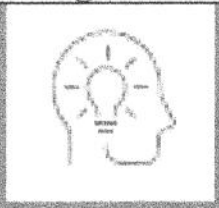

Launching your product as a private label and using FBA will ensure you are awarded the Prime badge and the buy box.

(2) Traffic

Advertise your offers—advertising will bring more eyeballs to your products and boost brand awareness. Refer to the Advertising chapter. Running deals or coupons is another way to promote your products. You can quickly learn to do this by following the instructions in SC; under the main menu, click "Advertising"—"Deals" and "Vouchers".

(3) Pricing

Set competitive prices—many customers shop for the best price. SC tools like automated repricing can help you stay competitive.

When you set up your listing, Amazon will ask you to provide a selling price range. Down the line—if you increase your selling price outside this range, Amazon might suppress your listing and not show it to customers immediately, as their computer systems "algorithm" might assume that there is a pricing error. You will then have to go through Seller Support ("SS") to get the price updated. Therefore, ensure that your price range is wide enough. For example, if you plan to sell a product for £40, provide a range from, say, £20 to £90 to give you flexibility to change the price.

(3.1)—Automated Pricing

Pricing is critical to Featured Offer ("buy box") eligibility on Amazon product detail pages. Amazon's automated pricing tool enables you to adjust your prices quickly and automatically against your competition, increasing your chances of converting more sales than the competition.

"Being selected as the Featured Offer can accelerate sales by up to 50%"—Amazon Internal Data, 2021.

Once you have automated pricing, you don't have to worry about managing prices and you can react to your competitors' price changes in real time. It only takes a few clicks to set up automate pricing. Search "automate pricing" in SC.

Your prices do not have to be consistently low. What I usually do is this—for an item that I want sell for £42 "target price", I will reduce it to £35 when my competition is selling at around £36 to £38. Then, after a day or two of selling at that price point, or after selling 200 units, I will increase the price to £40, i.e. above the competition. The temporary price reduction enables me to build momentum and climb the seller's rank ("seller authority"). After a week at £40, I will increase the price again to £42 and stay at £42. Customers will still buy my product based on the assumption that it's superior to the ones for £36 to £38. I will not sell as much as the competition, but will make much more profit per unit. When my inventory levels are high, my strategy is different. I'm happy with only a tiny margin and gaining a more significant market share—I see this as a way to invest in getting more reviews. The more reviews I get, the more and more sales I will make. Is it starting to sound like the flywheel yet?

The Perfect Launch

Speed matters in business. The first 90 days for Amazon sellers are especially critical for establishing marketing, fulfilment and pricing to accelerate performance beyond your first product launch. Amazon data scientists refer to the use of five selling programs. Sellers taking these five steps within that critical timeframe can generate sales more quickly, as many of the most successful sellers already have. Ready to join them? The playbook is simple:

(1) Brand Registry—enrol your brand in the Brand Registry. Refer to the Branding and Trademarks chapter;

(2) A+ Content—enhance your product detail pages with A+ Content. Refer to the SEO chapter;

(3) Use FBA;

(4) Automated Pricing—automate pricing on your offers;

(5) Advertising—run ads. Refer to the Advertising chapter.

10 SEARCH ENGINE OPTIMISATION ("SEO")

Amazon SEO is the process of optimising product listings to help them rank higher in product searches on Amazon. In other words, when a customer searches for products on Amazon, you want them to see your product at the top of the search results (list of products you see on your screen after a search on Amazon). Amazon SEO is a way of increasing the quantity and quality of traffic to your product listings through organic search results—appearing on search results without you having to pay for it through advertising. A few simple steps can improve listings for product search, boost sales, and help shoppers find your brand.

In this chapter, you will learn these essentials:

(1) How Amazon SEO works;

(2) How you can optimise your Amazon listings in 8 steps; and

(3) Four general Amazon SEO best practices

You can use SEO tactics to drive more traffic to your product listings, increase product and brand visibility, and boost conversion rates and sales growth.

Conversion rate—a conversion is the result of a customer taking action. The conversion rate is the percentage of customers that complete a purchase out of the total number of visitors to your product listing page. As more visitors buy products, the conversion rate goes up. Use the conversion rate as a Key Performance Indicator ("KPI") for measuring the impact of your SEO efforts.

How Amazon SEO works

These five items will help you understand how SEO works: (1) Amazon search box; (2) Search filters; (3) The search results page; (4) Sponsored products; and (5) Amazon sales rank.

(1) Amazon Search Box

Customers can search for items by typing a term or phrase into the search box at the top of the Amazon website or App. Online shoppers can use the Amazon search box to find products quickly with a drop-down menu of departments. Customers also have the option to type in general keywords. Amazon retrieves relevant results for the word or phrase, and the customer may refine the search to narrow down their search results.

(2) Search Filters

While searching for products, customers can use various filters to list search results in a specific order, including: (a) Department; (b) Best sellers—the most sold items; (c) New arrivals/new releases; (d) Featured items; (e) Customer reviews; (f) Movers and Shakers—the biggest gainers in sales rank over 24 hours; (g) High or low price; (h) Digital content and devices; and (i) Programs and features—for example, Subscribe and Save.

(3) The Search Results Page

Factors that can help determine search results include: (a)—Product titles; (b)—Product descriptions; (c)—Optimised images; (d)—Product features; and (e)—Competitive pricing.

You can use SEO to improve these elements to boost your ranking in Amazon search results.

The Listing Quality Dashboard is a widget on the SC home page. It is a tool that highlights specific product information that needs improvement and provides recommendations on which product attributes you should provide. This is Amazon's diagnostics of your product listing, which tells you which SEO tweaks you need to make to improve your selling performance—this is how Amazon tells you they love you.

(4) Sponsored Products

Sponsored Products are cost per click ("CPC") ads that sellers can use to promote individual product listings in Amazon stores; they are available to sellers with a professional selling account enrolled in the ABR. Ads appear within shopping results pages and on product detail pages. Amazon will automatically generate and match ads to shopping queries. Sponsored products can help you reach high-intent shoppers actively looking for products you've listed. Refer to the Advertising chapter.

(5) Amazon sales rank

Amazon gives all sellers a rating based on seller performance measurements, including: account health; reviews; and product price.

Generally, the higher you rank, the more selling potential you'll have. Sales rank is calculated based on all-time sales of an ASIN or product where recent sales are weighted more than older sales. Sales ranks are relative. While your product has had many sales, there may have been other products in the same category that have also seen an increase. Therefore, your rank might not improve much, even after a recent period of high sales volumes.

Optimise your Amazon listings in 8 steps

Think of SEO as a continual process to help you engage with Amazon's millions of customers. Start by making optimisation an ongoing part of your startup's strategy. You must also focus your efforts on seven parts of a product listing as below:

(1) Keywords;

(2) Product titles;

(3) Product images;
(4) Product descriptions;
(5) Key features—bullet points on a product listing page;
(6) Backend search keywords,
(7) Product pricing; and
(8) A/B testing.

Let's dive into how to improve each of these elements from an SEO standpoint.

Step 1: Conduct Keyword Research

Compile a comprehensive list of keywords. Keywords are the words and phrases people use when searching for something online. Think about the products that you are planning to launch and put yourself in the customer's shoes:

(a) What words or phrases would you type into the Amazon search box to find your product?
(b) How do customers find products like yours?

To figure out what keywords to incorporate into your SEO strategy, give these ideas a try—type a variety of words and phrases in the Amazon search box. Then, look at the drop-down suggestions and start compiling a list of relevant keywords for similar listings. For example, results for "blackout curtains" are in the screenshot below:

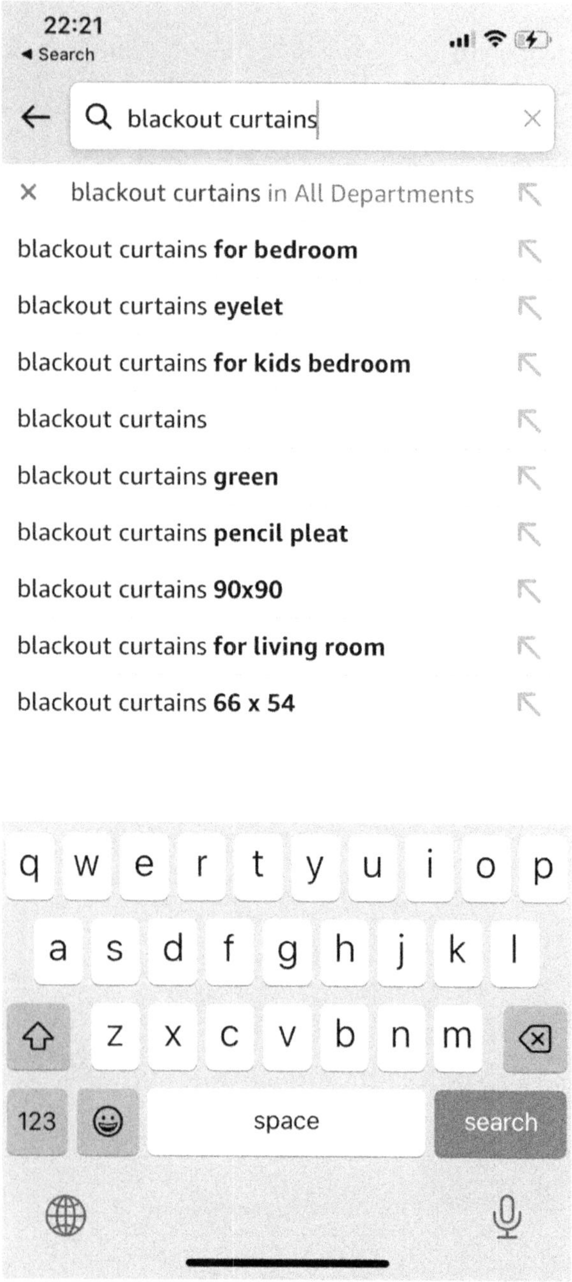
22:21
Search
blackout curtains
blackout curtains in All Departments
blackout curtains for bedroom
blackout curtains eyelet
blackout curtains for kids bedroom
blackout curtains
blackout curtains green
blackout curtains pencil pleat
blackout curtains 90x90
blackout curtains for living room
blackout curtains 66 x 54
q w e r t y u i o p
a s d f g h j k l
z x c v b n m
123
space
search

(c) Use competitor results—type in your competitors' product details, such as brand name and product title and see what Amazon suggests.
(d) While compiling your list, differentiate between short-tail and long-tail keywords:
Short-tail keywords are broader searches with high search volume and competition. They may have lower conversion because the customer is browsing for different options, for example, "blackout curtains".
Long-tail keywords are relatively specific. They typically have low search volume, low competition, and a higher conversion rate, because customers know precisely what they want, for example, "cotton, 2m x 2m, green blackout curtains".

Both types of keywords are necessary as part of your SEO strategy. Customers typing in long-tail keywords are commonly looking for particular products. You can use long-tail keywords to capture these more precise purchases. Short-tail keywords can attract visibility to your brand, but it can also be challenging to rank for these less specific, more competitive terms.
(e) The auto-complete feature on the Amazon search box is a great way to find popular long-tail keywords related to your product.

Step 2: Optimise the Product Title

You only have a moment to catch a customer's attention. The product title is one of the primary fields used by Amazon and search engines to measure the relevance of a product page as part of a customer search. There are a few things you can do to increase the chances of a customer clicking on your product title:
(a) Your product title should match what would be on the physical packaging of your product;
(b) Pay attention to title length—Amazon recommends approximately 60 characters and a maximum of 80 characters. Longer titles are more challenging to read, so the longer your title is, the more you risk losing a customer's attention;
(c) Pay attention to the different title lengths along with preferred title styles for listings in each product category;

(d) Do not use all caps—instead use title case, whereby you capitalise the first letter of each word, except for prepositions, for example, (in, on, over, with), conjunctions (and, or, for), or articles (the, a, an);
(e) Begin a title with the product's brand name, in addition to ensuring the brand name field is populated in the backend of your product detail page;
(f) Use numerals: "2" instead of "two."
(g) Don't use non-language ASCII characters such as Æ, ©, or ®;
(h) Titles should contain the minimal information needed to identify the item and nothing more.
(i) Don't use subjective commentary, such as "hot item" or "best seller";
(j) Titles can include necessary punctuation, like hyphens (-), forward slashes (/), commas (,), ampersands (&), and periods (.); and
(k) Titles can abbreviate measurements, such as "cm", "oz", "in", and "kg".

Apply the guidance above to ensure you appear in relevant searches and avoid search suppression. Amazon will not offer customers your products if your listing does not comply with the requirements above.

Use the brand field—while the brand name is often contained in the title, description, and bullet points, you should also include it in the brand field. If customers filter by brand and your listing is missing the brand designation—even if it is included in the description—customers may never find your listing.

Step 3: Optimise Product Images

Quality images help customers visually evaluate and compare key features. Multiple images enable them to see your product from different angles, and can persuade a customer to choose one search result over another. Images should also show your product in use and highlight different features. Here are some factors to bear in mind when listing your products and putting together your product images:

(a) Every product detail page requires at least one product image. Six images and one video are ideal;

(b) Images should be clear, informative, and attractive;

(c) The main images should have a white background and fill at least 85% of the image space

(d) Use 500 x 500 or 1,000 x 1,000 pixels to increase listing quality.

Evaluate your image quality based on these guidelines:

(a) The image matches the product description in size, colour, and accuracy;

(b) The product is recognisable;

(c) The image is a photo and not a drawing;

(d) The photo is taken at a flattering angle;

(e) The product is focused and well-lit;

(f) Highlights/shadows do not obscure close-up shots;

(g) The entire product is depicted in the image;

(h) Backgrounds are simple and clean, so as not to distract from the product

(i) Provide as many different images as possible. Many product categories allow for the inclusion of alternate images.

Optimise images in the Seller App—use the "Product Photo Studio" to edit your listing photos. Access this feature under the main menu or from the top left on the main page. This feature offers automatic and manual image exposure or brightness adjustment, cropping and turning the background white.

Step 4: Optimise Product Descriptions

Use detailed product features and usage information in high-quality product descriptions to help customers find, evaluate, and purchase your products. You can also highlight specific product information not located elsewhere in the listing. Here are more

tips for creating high-quality product descriptions:
(a) Include brand names;
(b) Include sizes—for example, if selling shoes or clothes, include the different sizes for the UK, the US, the EU etc.;
(c) Include material type, for example, canvas/leather for a backpack; and
(d) Mention relevant details such as colours, packaging, and quantity.

For additional details on best practices for a good quality listing, refer to the Product Listing chapter.

Use A+ Content

A+ Content enables brands to describe product features in new ways by including a unique brand story, enhanced images and text placements, which may result in higher conversion rates, increased traffic and increased sales.

Additional benefits of A+ Content include brands being able to showcase product features with: (1) technical specs, (2) comparative product information; (3) Additional rich content, including images; and (4) product set-up/unboxing videos. For example, the link "www.amazon.co.uk/dp/B0CHXFCYCR" shows an example of a product listing and A+ Content for an iPhone 15.

"Adding A+ content to detail pages can help increase sales by an average of 5.6%"—Amazon Internal Data, 2020

Step 5: Optimise Product Key Features

Key features—these are the bullet points on a product listing page; they also factor into the relevance of a detail page as part of a customer search. Well-written bullet points will naturally contain keywords, but the priority should be to communicate clearly and help customers make a buying decision. One approach is to start your bullet points with a feature and then state the benefits of that feature—be clear and concise. Use the following guidelines as you craft your bullet points:
(5.1) Include up to five bullet points for each product;
(5.2) Keep your bullet points under 1,000 characters for all five bullets. This guideline improves readability. Bullet points are not always indexed by Amazon search, but they always appear in full on product detail pages;

(5.3) Highlight the five key features you want customers to know about your product, such as: (a) dimensions; (b) age appropriateness; (c) ideal conditions for the product; (d) skill level; and (e) contents.
(5.4) Maintain a consistent order. If your first bullet point is country of origin, keep that exact order for all products—this is relevant for products with variations;
(5.5) Reinforce important information from the title and description;
(5.6) Begin each bullet point with a capital letter;
(5.7) Write with sentence fragments and do not include ending punctuation; and
(5.8) Do not include promotional and pricing information.

Product Key Features Examples

Here's an example of an essential bulleted list that follows the guidelines for describing a set of rain gear:
(a) Drawstring-adjustable hood and snap-adjustable cuffs to keep you dry;
(b) Roomy, comfortable fit suitable for any season;
(c) 100% waterproof for rainy weather protection;
(d) Breathable to keep you cool in the dampest conditions and
(e) Available in khaki, yellow, or green colours.

Besides these general guidelines, each category has a templated guideline. To learn more, download the guide templates from SC, by searching: "inventory templates for product categories" in SC.

Bullet points are an effective way to sell your product's key features and benefits. Customers rely on them to understand a product's essential/distinguishing characteristics. They enhance the customer experience—and my own testing has shown that well-crafted bullet points increase sales. See the A/B Testing section below.

Step 6: Optimise Product Search Terms

Search terms are backend keywords that allow you to create engaging and readable content for a product page while ensuring

that Amazon indexes all relevant keywords.
Customers do not see these search terms, so adding them to the "backend" of product listings further enhances the discoverability of products.
Tips for optimising your search terms:
(a) Only include generic words;
(b) Include synonyms, abbreviations, and alternative names for a product;
(c) Stay under the length limit—you have less than 250 bytes, so minimise unnecessary characters. Spaces and punctuation don't count;
(d) When entering phrases, type them in a logical order of search;
(e) Include spelling variations if applicable, but don't deliberately include common misspellings;
(f) Include abbreviations and alternate names;
(g) You can use all lower-case letters;
(h) You don't need any punctuation, so skip hyphens (-), colons (:), and so forth;
(i) Separate words with spaces only;
(j) Don't repeat words within the search terms field;
(k) No need for stop words such as "a," "an," "and," "by," "for," "of," "the," "with," etc.;
(l) Use singular or plural; there is no need for both.

How to add Search Terms through your Amazon Seller Central account
Step 1—Sign into SC;
Step 2—Under Inventory, click "Manage Inventory";
Step 3—Find the relevant listing and click, "Edit";
Step 4—Select the "Keywords" tab; and
Step 5—Enter your search terms in the "Search terms" field and save.

Lean into Brand Analytics ("BA")—use the brand analytics search terms report called "the BA report" to enhance your keywords and optimise your listings. The BA report is of great benefit to brand owners. It shows them how customers, in aggregate, find branded and competitor products on Amazon. It shows the most popular search terms during a given period, each term's search frequency rank and the top three products that customers clicked on after searching.

Brand owners can look up a specific term to see the products that aggregate customers are clicking on after searching for that term; or they can search for a particular product to establish which terms are driving aggregate customers to click on that product.

Step 7: Optimise Product Price

The price of products can influence conversion rates and sales growth. To price products competitively, research the competition and adjust—develop a compelling price point within your niche. Use Amazon's automated pricing tool to optimise prices.

Step 8: A/B Testing

Optimising your content with the "Manage Your Experiment" or the A/B Testing Tool—a widget on the SC home page—*"can help drive an average of an additional £13k in annual revenue"*—Amazon Internal Data

Use the tool to compare product images, titles, and A+ Content to determine the content that drives more sales.

A/B testing—also known as split tests, lets you compare two versions of content, to see which performs better. You can use A/B testing to learn how to build better content that appeals to your customers and drive sales. The minimum time you can run the test for is four weeks, so you must be patient. This allows Amazon to gather sufficient data to determine which version performs better. You can auto-publish the "winning" version when the experiment is complete. This is a great feature. I started using it in 2022 to optimise product titles, images and product key features ("bullet points"). The A/B testing tool can also be accessed through the main menu—click "Brands" — "Manage Experiences" or search "A/B testing" in SC.

The Four General Amazon SEO best practices are: (1) Don't repeat keywords; (2) Answer the customers' questions; (3) Improve your rankings; and (4) Basic style tips for listings.

1. Don't Repeat Keywords

Focus on providing a positive customer experience. Write naturally and focus on giving customers the information they need to purchase. Keyword repetition or keyword stuffing is counterproductive as it works against you.

Keyword stuffing—the repeated use of the exact keywords in content.

Don't risk losing customers by using keyword stuffing as an SEO tactic. It's an ineffective and outdated strategy that could harm your search engine rankings. Instead, create high-quality, engaging content that resonates with your target audience. Doing so will improve your search engine rankings, and thus attract and retain more customers in the long run. Remember, quality beats quantity every time.

2. Answer the Customers' Questions

Answer customer questions and product inquiries on your product page. Focus on what your customer would want to know about a product, as opposed to what you want to say about it.

3. Help Improve Your Rankings

There are various ways to increase your Amazon ranking. By maintaining Amazon standards, you are in a better position to connect with potential customers. Generally, the higher you rank, the more selling potential you'll have.

(a) Optimise your product listing, including title, product descriptions, key features, images, and pricing;

(b) Positive reviews improve your search ranking. Refer to the Customer Reviews chapter;

(c) Use FBA and ensure you are displaying the "Amazon Prime badge";

(d Use A+ Content;

(e) Track your product ranking on the Brand Analytics Dashboard;

(f) Use Amazon Selling Coach—a tool that diagnoses your account and provides recommendations on how to improve your sales. Sometimes, recommendations will occasionally pop up on your SC dashboard/home page; don't ignore them.

4. Use these Basic Style Tips for Listings

(a) Be descriptive but clear and concise.

(b) Be persuasive but not pushy/gimmicky.

(c) Be accurate and truthful about your product's condition and quality. This avoids terrible reviews.

(d) Avoid making exaggerated or subjective claims.

Improving your Amazon SEO game will drive product visibility, boost sales and enhance the customer shopping experience.

Amazon SEO Tools—the tools discussed in this chapter, such as A+ Content, The Listing Quality Dashboard, the A/B testing, and Seller University, will help scale your startup.

Seller University—offers educational resources and tools to learn and grow as a seller. Search "Seller University" in SC.

11 CUSTOMER REVIEWS

Customer reviews help customers learn more about your products and decide whether or not to purchase them. Customer reviews should give potential customers genuine product feedback from fellow shoppers. Amazon has a zero-tolerance policy for any review designed to mislead or manipulate customers—and they don't allow anyone to write reviews as a form of promotion. The following are types of reviews that Amazon does not allow; they will thus be removed:
(1) A review by someone who has a direct or indirect financial interest in your product;
(2) A review by someone perceived to have a close personal relationship with you;
(3) A review by the product manufacturer, posing as an unbiased customer;
(4) Multiple negative reviews for the same product from one customer;
(5) A review in exchange for monetary reward; and
(6) A negative review from a seller on a competitor's product.

Amazon Verified Purchase Reviews

Amazon Verified Purchase Reviews—Amazon has verified that the person who wrote the review purchased the product on Amazon and didn't receive the product at a significant discount. Reviews that are not marked Amazon Verified Purchase are valuable as well, but this means that Amazon was not able to confirm that the product was purchased on Amazon, or that the customer paid a price that is available to most Amazon customers.

Amazon Vine Programme

Amazon Vine invites the most trusted reviewers on Amazon to post opinions about new products and help fellow customers make informed purchase decisions. They also invite buyers to become Vine reviewers—also known as Vine Voices, based on the insightfulness of the reviews they published on their Amazon purchases.

A new seller who wants to participate must provide a few free units of their products for this selected group of Vine Voices to post product reviews. The Vine Programme enables new sellers to build awareness for their products, boost sales of their slow and kick start ASINs. Here are some prerequisites before you can participate in Vine—you must be: (1) a professional selling partner; (2) the brand owner; (3) using FBA; and (4) an authorised brand representative in the ABR.

Once your enrolment is complete, Vine Voices can request your enrolled products to review. After the first Vine review has been published, you will be charged a one-off £140—at the time of print. The enrolment fee is charged per parent ASIN. For example, a product that comes in three different sizes or colours will only be charged £140. You will not be charged a fee if the enrolled product receives no reviews within 90 days.

In addition to the requirements above, you must also meet the following criteria: (1) have less than 30 reviews on the product detail page; (2) not be offering second-hand and or adult products; (3) you have already launched your products at the time of Vine enrolment; (4) you have FBA inventory; and (5) you have a fully completed listing.

Products are excluded from Vine if they are required to be bundled into multiple products for delivery and require the reviewers to order another product separately to conduct a review.

Alternative Methods for Getting More Reviews

The following strategies can also help you get reviews faster, so we will discuss each one in detail: (1) Lower prices to boost sales volume; (2) Request reviews directly from customers; (3) Give customers an option to provide "One Tap Review(s)"; (4) Engage with your customers and (5) Enable global review sharing.

(1) Lower Prices

"Some brands adjust prices to secure more reviews. For example, Arçelik is a Turkish producer of white goods and other appliances, which it offers under various sub-brands. It sells just one of those brands, Grundig, via online platforms such as Amazon. When selling in brick-and-mortar stores, Arçelik typically unveils a new product at a high price point and then begins discounting only if sales are slow. When it began selling its Grundig appliances on Amazon, it quickly learned that the opposite strategy could make sense. "Online, we start with a low price to get consumers to buy and leave reviews, and then we increase the price of the items with good ratings," says Noyan Ceritoğlu, Arçelik's e-commerce manager."—Harvard Business Review

(2) Use the "Request a Review" feature provided by Amazon in SC

Amazon doesn't require you to request reviews because they do that on your behalf—in an email asking customers to rate your product using a five-point system as follows:

5 stars—Excellent;
4 stars—Good;
3 stars—Fair;
2 stars—Poor; and
1 star—Awful.

However, Amazon allows you to send review requests for specific orders using the "Request a review" feature on the "Order Details" page in SC, instead of asking for reviews using email or through the "Buyer-Seller Messaging" tool, also in SC. When you request a review using "Request a review", Amazon will ask for a product review and seller feedback for the order in the same email. These requests use standardised language and are automatically translated into the customer's preferred language.

You can use this feature to request reviews once for each order, between 5 and 30 days after the delivery date. This ensures that customers receive relevant and recent review requests. To request a review, using the "Request a review" feature, log into

SC, from the main menu click "Orders"—"Manage Orders"; "View FBA Orders"—click on orders that say "Payment complete" in the "Order Status" column—"Request Review"; finally, click "Yes" to confirm that you want to send the review. This can be a time-consuming process if you have many orders for which you want to request reviews. The process can be automated using a Jungle Scout Google Chrome Extension. Google "Jungle Scout FBA review automation".

(3) One Tap Review

One of the main reasons that many customers don't provide product feedback is the amount of time it takes to describe what they like or don't like about the product. One Tap Review allows customers to give a star rating for a product without writing a detailed review—aiming to dramatically streamline the customer review process, encouraging those with little time or motivation to review their purchases.

(4) Engage with Your Customers

Building long-term relationships and engaging with your customers can help lead to more reviews. When someone buys from you repeatedly and loves what you sell, they are naturally encouraged to leave positive feedback for your products. One way to engage with customers is to answer their questions on your product listings.

Another way to engage with your audience is to find Amazon Associates affiliate program members who promote products and encourage them to use your products and follow up with a review request. If they have liked your products, they are likely to leave reviews, as they make their money through a commission made after customers make a purchase based on their recommendations—it's like using Instagram influencers, but on Amazon. This will also help boost the popularity of your products, allowing you to convert most of the traffic they send to your listing.

(5) Global Review Sharing

As you expand into other countries on Amazon, sell your product using the same ASIN, brand name and SC account. This way, reviews from each marketplace are shared across all marketplaces—in different countries. With global review sharing, reviews on your UK marketplace will be shown on, for example, amazon.com and amazon.de and vice versa.

Without global review sharing, only reviews from the country where the customer views the product are displayed. In other words, as a new seller selling only on Amazon.co.uk, you won't have global reviews. You can use this feature after you have expanded into international markets. Below is an example which shows how international reviews are displayed on a product detail page:

00:45
◂ Search
Search Amazon.co.uk
Perfect for beginners and advanced tailors. Heavy duty always best choose for all kind of sawing.
One person found this helpful
Helpful
Report
See all reviews
Top reviews from other countries
Translate all reviews to English
Cliente Amazon
Verified Purchase
Máquina excelente! Vale o investimento!
Reviewed in Brazil on 26 January 2022
Tudo o que eu esperava e muito mais! Ela realmente consegue costurar várias camadas de tecido (lembrando que tem que trocar a agulha!). O botão de play/pausa é muito útil. Ela vem com muitos acessórios, alguns que não acompanham outras máquinas de outras linhas da Singer ou...
See more
7 people found this helpful
Add to Basket
Report
6

12 ADVERTISING

This is one of the most extensive and essential chapters in this book—so grab your coffee, or whatever else you need to do, and ensure you are 100% focused—before we strap ourselves in!
Increase Visibility and Sales through Amazon Advertising
Now, you understand that you pay Amazon a commission—a referral fee for every sale you make and for storing and shipping your products to customers—annoyingly, you will also have to pay them for advertising,. Below are some advertising insights:

+40% increase in units ordered
"ASINs saw an average weekly +40% lift in units ordered within the first year after launching a sponsored products campaign"—Amazon Internal Data, WW, 2019

+54% increase in glance views
"ASINs saw an average weekly +54% lift in glance views within the first year after launching a sponsored products campaign"—Amazon Internal Data, WW, 2019

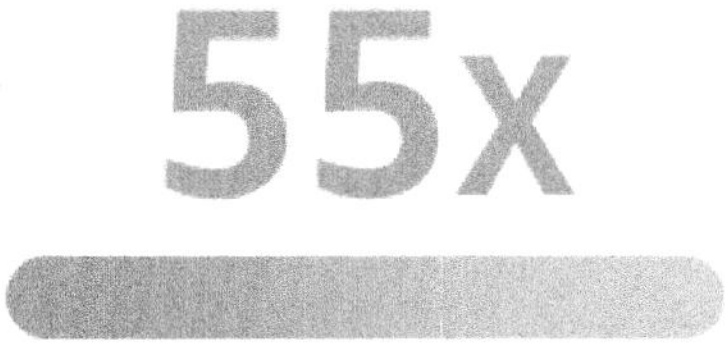

55X increase in impressions
"Adding three or more bullet points to your product page and advertising with sponsored products can help you increase impressions by 55X"—Compared to products that did not take this action over the same period—Amazon Internal Data, US & UK, All Product Lines, January – July 2020

93X more unit sales
"Adding A+ content to your detail page and advertising with sponsored products can help generate up to 93X more unit sales"—Compared to products that did not take this action over the same period—Amazon Internal Data, US & UK, All Product Lines, January – July 2020

The rest of this chapter is structured as follows:

(1) Four campaign types

(1.1) Sponsored products

(1.2) Sponsored brands

(1.3) Sponsored display

(1.4) Stores

(2) What you need to start advertising

(3) Targeting options

(4) How to manage and structure your campaigns

My ad campaigns are structured like in the table below. It's fine if the table doesn't make sense at this point—go through the chapter and come back to this table to connect the dots:

SELL £250K IN 18 MONTHS ON AMAZON

Campaign types	**Targeting options**	**Targeting strategy**		**My strategy**
Sponsored products	Automatic	Close match		Dynamic bid down only
		Loose match		N/A
		Substitutes		N/A
		Compliments		N/A
	Manual	Keyword targeting	Broad match	N/A
			Phrase match	Dynamic bid down only
			Exact match	Dynamic bid down only
		Product targeting	Specific products	Specific ASINs
			Product category	N/A
	Negative	Keyword targeting	Broad match	Keyword targeting
			Phrase match	Keyword targeting
			Exact match	Keyword targeting
		Product targeting		Specific ASINs

Campaign types	**Targeting options**	**Targeting strategy**		**My strategy**
Sponsored brands	Manual	Keyword targeting	Broad match	Dynamic bid up to 10%
			Phrase match	Dynamic bid up to 10%
			Exact match	Dynamic bid up to 10%
Sponsored display	N/A			
Store	N/A			

(1) Four Campaign Types

Sponsored ads can help you boost your visibility, reach more customers, and increase sales. Advertising on Amazon can be achieved through running these four types of campaigns: (1) Sponsored products; (2) Sponsored brands; (3) Sponsored display; and (4) Stores.

(1.1) Sponsored Products

Sponsored products are CPC ads that promote individual product listings on Amazon. You can create a campaign in just a few minutes, even if you've never advertised. Sponsored products appear within shopping results pages and on product detail pages. They can help you reach high-intent shoppers actively looking for products like yours. The screenshot below is an example of a sponsored products campaign on Amazon after searching for "blackout curtains"; this can be identified by the word "Sponsored" on the top of the listing:

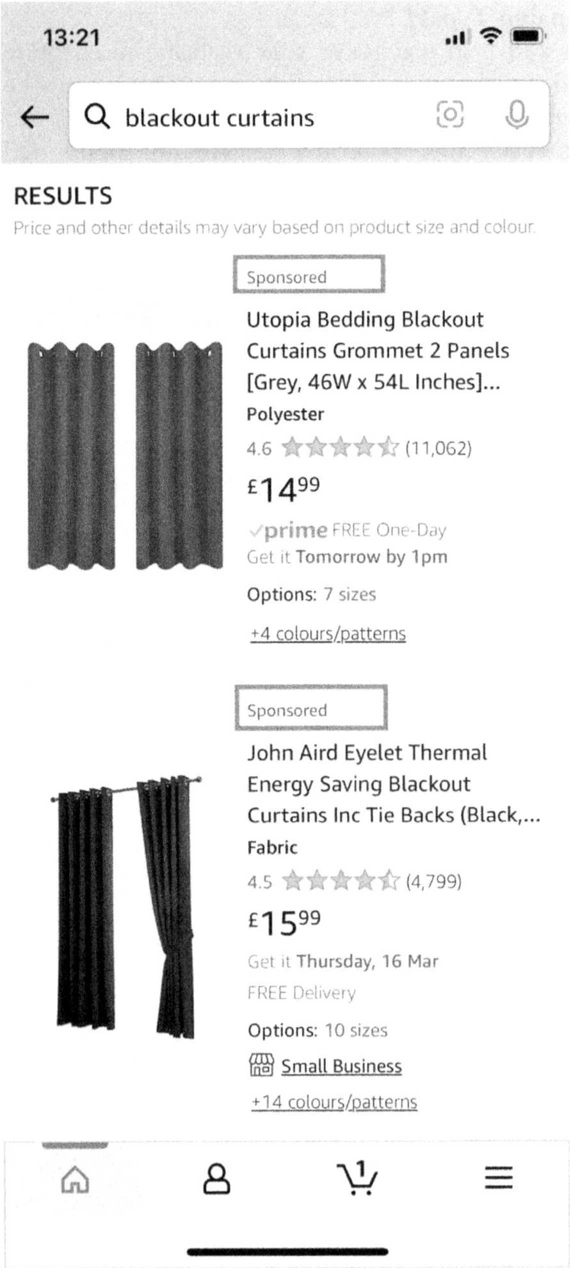
13:21
blackout curtains
RESULTS
Price and other details may vary based on product size and colour.
Sponsored
Utopia Bedding Blackout Curtains Grommet 2 Panels [Grey, 46W x 54L Inches]...
Polyester
4.6 (11,062)
£14.99
prime FREE One-Day
Get it Tomorrow by 1pm
Options: 7 sizes
+4 colours/patterns
Sponsored
John Aird Eyelet Thermal Energy Saving Blackout Curtains Inc Tie Backs (Black,...
Fabric
4.5 (4,799)
£15.99
Get it Thursday, 16 Mar
FREE Delivery
Options: 10 sizes
Small Business
+14 colours/patterns

Familiarise yourself with these advertising terms:

Cost per click ("CPC")—this is a metric that determines how much advertisers pay for the ads they place on search results pages for search engines, websites or social media Apps—based on the ad's number of clicks. It's a metric that applies to all types of ads, whether they have text, images or videos. As a seller, your goal is to reduce the price of clicks, while cultivating high-quality clicks and consequently, having more satisfied customers.

How to calculate the CPC—it equals the average amount paid for each click on an ad. Thus it is total ad spend divided by the number of clicks. A high number of clicks or visits on an ad means that the ad is getting attention from customers. Various advertisers can bid on ad placement on websites and popular keywords. So, each brand's optimal CPC is determined by its ad ranking and the ranking of other related brands and products. The more in-demand a keyword is in the auction, the higher the ad placement and the higher the ad spend.

The "maximum cost per click" is your bid on ad placement and keywords, which means it's the highest price you're willing to pay. Unless you have set up your Amazon ad campaigns to go above your bid price per click, you will typically not pay the entire maximum cost per click, the actual CPC will often be lower than that initial bid.

What is manual cost-per-click bidding—you must determine if you want to use manual or automatic cost-per-click bidding. Manual cost-per-click bidding means that you choose your bid amounts. Automatic cost-per-click uses enhanced cost-per-click bidding, in other words, Amazon determines the correct level of bid based on demand for the keyword that you are bidding for. With enhanced cost-per-click bidding, you set your overall budget and then have your bids automated by Amazon.

Enhanced cost-per-click bidding is a feature added to search engines, including Google AdWords and Microsoft Bing. CPM—is the cost per thousand, also known as cost per thousand impressions or cost per mile. It's a formula that calculates the total ad spend per 1,000 impressions on a web page.

Pay-per-click ("PPC") vs CPC

PPC and CPC describe the same thing—PPC is the system by which you end up paying per click on an ad. CPC is the metric used to measure those clicks.

There are upsides and downsides to PPC advertising, which CPC and CPM measure—CPC is more directly correlated to the purchases made by customers, while CPM could help reach the goal of increasing brand awareness. This will often result in CPC advertising being higher priced and more valuable in getting customers to the next step in their shopping journey, since CPC is directly linked to the click-through rate ("CTR") of customers who have viewed your ads.

Your goal is to have a low CPC. That means that ads should have optimisation for high conversation at a low cost. Additionally, CPC should be proportionate to the overall profits of your brand/products since the goal of CPC is to drive sales. You do not want to spend more on ads than your income—therefore, budgeting is crucial

(1.2) Sponsored Brands

Sponsored brands showcase your brand and product portfolio. Featuring your brand logo, a custom headline, and a selection of your products, these ads appear on shopping results pages, helping drive sales and product visibility.

Sponsored brands allow you to quickly grow consideration for your brand from customers who have expressed an interest in products like yours. The mobile screenshot below shows how sponsored brand ads on Amazon for the brands—Phillips and Braun.

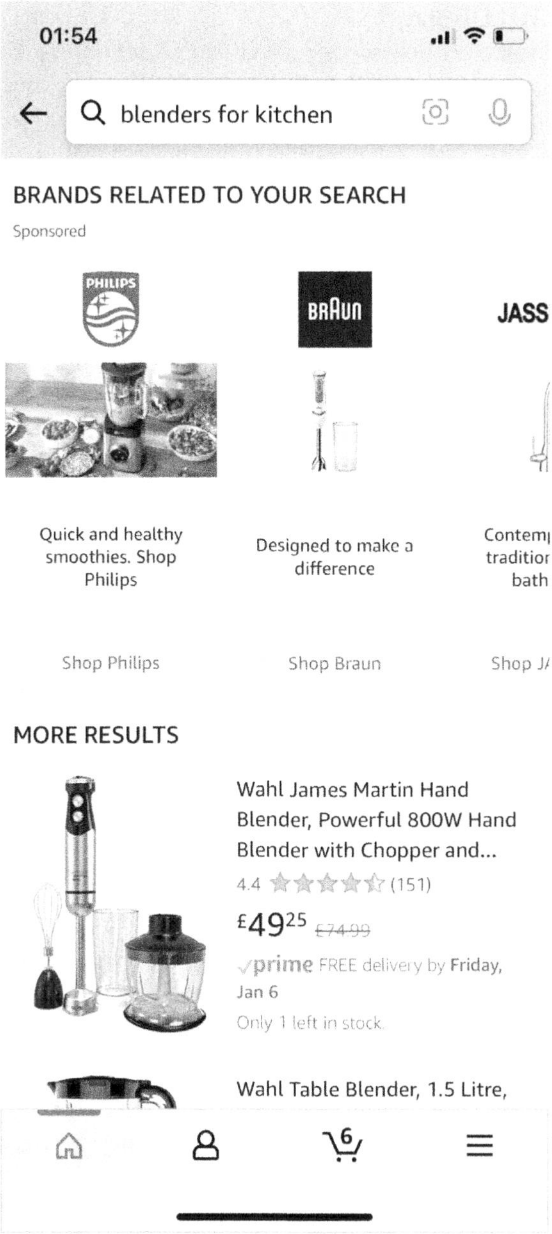
01:54
blenders for kitchen
BRANDS RELATED TO YOUR SEARCH
Sponsored
PHILIPS
BRAUN
JASS
Quick and healthy smoothies. Shop Philips
Designed to make a difference
Contem
traditior
bath
Shop Philips
Shop Braun
Shop J
MORE RESULTS
Wahl James Martin Hand Blender, Powerful 800W Hand Blender with Chopper and...
4.4 (151)
£49.25 £74.99
prime FREE delivery by Friday, Jan 6
Only 1 left in stock.
Wahl Table Blender, 1.5 Litre,
6

(1.3) Sponsored Display

Sponsored display is a self-service advertising solution that helps advertisers reach relevant audiences across the shopper journey with ad placements that appear both on and off Amazon. Sponsored display can help you reach audiences beyond those actively shopping on Amazon.

With sponsored display, you can reach customers who previously viewed your brand's product detail pages and encourage them to return to those pages. When shoppers click your sponsored display ads, they're taken to your product detail page, store or a custom landing page displaying your products.

Sponsored display ads are expensive—it's hard to convert customers who might not yet be ready to make a purchase. These customers have to be brought to Amazon from somewhere else like Instagram, Facebook or Google. There is also the risk that you will lose these customers to other sellers. Amazon will encourage you to use sponsored display ads, so that you can pay for the cost of bringing these customers to them. Whether the customers ends up buying from you or your competitors—it's a win for Amazon—as they will get their commission either way.

Don't get me wrong, I am not saying that sponsored display ads don't work. It is harder to quantify their benefits, as customers you introduce to your brand today might not buy your product immediately but in the future. If I were starting today, I wouldn't use sponsored display until I have mastered sponsored products and brands.

(1.4) Stores

Stores are custom multipage shopping destinations on Amazon for individual brands that let you showcase your brand story and product offering. They require no website experience to use, and they are free. With stores, you can choose from a rich set of easy-to-create content templates and tiles, rearrange them with easy drag-and-drop functionality, and make a professional-looking website—your very own Amazon store—without coding or design skills.

(2) —What You Need to Start Advertising

Account—you must have an active professional seller account—in addition, to use sponsored display, sponsored brands and stores, you need to be enrolled in the Amazon Brand Registry.

Featured Offer—the products you advertise with sponsored products must be eligible for featured offer ("Buy Box") —this is not an issue for FBA sellers. Refer to the Selling Vehicles/Selling Models chapter.

Products—at the time of print, Amazon does not allow sellers to advertise adult, used and/refurbished products.

> Focus on sponsored products and brands—they are the most effective. The best I have achieved is a 35% ACOS for sponsored display and stores over a three-year period. To put this into perspective—if you sell a product for £100, you will spend £35 for each sale. This is expensive and not sustainable. With sponsored products and brands, the ACOS is well below 20%. I suggest you stick to sponsored products and brands for the first 12 months and try the other advertising methods after gaining some experience. For the past two years, my best-performing ads have been sponsored brand ads that auto-play videos on the search results pages; before that, they were sponsored products—automatic and manual phrase match campaigns. If you really need to, you can still test sponsored display ads and stores; but start with a meagre budget compared to sponsored products and brands

The focus of this book will be sponsored product advertising—other ad types also work well; however, they can be costly, especially when you have just launched.

Keep running your sponsored product ads; you will see that the ACOS will come down as you get more reviews—improving your sales velocity and seller authority.

(3) Targeting

The table below is a visual presentation of how the targeting section is structured and won't make much sense at this point.

Go through the section and come back to the table to connect the dots:

Targeting options	**Targeting strategy**		**Bidding strategy**
Automatic		Close match	Dynamic bids etc.
			Fixed bids etc.
		Loose match	
		Substitutes	
		Compliments	
Manual	Keyword targeting	Broad match	
		Phrase match	
		Exact match	
	Product targeting	Specific products	
		Product categories	
Negative	Keyword targeting	Keywords	
	Product targeting	ASINs	

What is targeting and why is it important? Robust targeting is crucial to build a solid foundation for sponsored product ads, and can help match shoppers' intentions to your products. Targeting is how you define the context in which you want your ads to appear. That can be done in multiple ways. The most common is using keywords that match your ad with customer shopping queries when looking for something online. For example, if you sell "2m x 2m green blackout curtains", you can target the keywords "green blackout curtains"—customers who type in "green blackout curtains" in Amazon search will be shown your "2m x 2m green blackout curtain".

Targeting Options

With sponsored products, you have three targeting options:

(1) Automatic targeting;

(2) Manual targeting; and

(3) Negative targeting.

Automatic Targeting

With automatic targeting—your ad is automatically matched with keywords that Amazon considers relevant to the products you are advertising. It is based on previous shopping queries and your product information. This targeting option can help you launch a new campaign easily and quickly. If you are a seasoned advertiser, it can help you understand search trends and serve as a source of keyword discovery for manual campaigns.

Manual targeting

With manual targeting, you can manually select the keywords or products you want to target. For products that you target—your ads will pop up either at the top, bottom or sides of the product listing page targeted.

Negative targeting

Negative targeting helps you exclude the keywords, products and brands you don't want associated with your ads. It will help you optimise your campaign's performance and spending. It can be used in both automatic and manual campaigns. You can add negative targets when setting up the campaign for the first time, or later, after determining the keywords that cost you a lot but with very little or no sales. In the first month of automatic targeting, list any keywords that are leading customers to your listing but never make a purchase, for example, a keyword with 30 clicks but no sale—add these as negative keywords. To add negative keywords or products to your campaigns, log into in SC, under the main menu, click—"Advertising"—"Campaigns"—click on the campaign you want to add negative keywords or products to—click "Negative keywords" or "Negative targeting"—"Add negative keywords" or "Add negative product targets"—and add your negative keywords or ASINs for product targeting.

Proactively tweak, adjust bids and add negative keywords to your ads in the first month, to lower your ad spend. For the first one to four months, review the performance of your automatic campaigns daily and add any negative keywords that you discover. The search term report that Amazon provides will show you the irrelevant terms that customers have used that you have paid for and can be avoided in future.

(3.1) Automatic Targeting Strategies

With automatic targeting, your ads will be eligible to appear on Amazon's shopping results and product detail pages. This is based on multiple default strategies that Amazon use on your behalf to match your ads to relevant customers' shopping queries. There are four automatic targeting strategies: (1) Close match; (2) Loose match; (3) Substitutes; and (4) Complements. Let's dive into these strategies:

Close match—Amazon shows your ad to shoppers who use search terms closely related to your products. If your product is a "Kitchen Smart – Large Espresso Stainless Steel Maker", Amazon will show your ad when shoppers use search terms like "large espresso maker" and "stainless steel espresso machine".

Loose match—Amazon shows your ad to shoppers who use search terms loosely related to your products. If your product is a "Kitchen Smart – Large Espresso Stainless Steel Maker", Amazon will show your ad when shoppers use search terms like "coffee machine" and "large silver espresso machine".

Substitutes—Amazon shows your ad to shoppers browsing detail pages of products similar to yours. If your product is a "Kitchen Smart--Espresso Maker, Stainless Steel, Metallic", Amazon will show your ad on detail pages that include "Coffee Ltd Espresso Machine" and "Ceramic Black Coffee Maker".

Complements—Amazon shows your ad to shoppers who view the detail pages of products that complement your product. If your product is a "Kitchen Smart--Espresso Maker, Stainless Steel, Metallic". Amazon will show your ad on detail pages that include "coffee bean" and "espresso mug".

Close match has been the most effective strategy throughout my campaigns in the past couple of years. The other targeting strategies resulted in an ACOS that was too high, therefore I've stopped using them

When to choose automatic targeting?

Automatic targeting ads are an excellent way to start for new sellers as they are perfect when:

(1) You're launching a new product and want to discover insights on shopping searches;

(2) You want to identify new keywords that drive clicks and sales that you can add to your manual campaigns; and

(3) You want to expand reach, to find more customers, and want a campaign that will dynamically adapt to changing trends and seasonality.

Let's re-cap—if I were starting as a new seller today, I would only run sponsored products for a month. Amazon recommends letting your automatic campaign run for about two weeks before creating a manual campaign. I suggest even longer—up to a month—so that you get as much precise information as possible. At the end of each month, Amazon cleanses the ads data before they can bill you a final invoice for that month. Their data is more accurate after their month-end billing.

So after your one month of automatic ads, I would create new manual ads. I will still keep the best-performing automatic ads running, and keep adding new negative keywords to both campaign types as I discover them—automatic targeting is an excellent supplement to manual campaigns.

(3.2) Manual Targeting

Manual targeting can be split into two categories: (1) keywords targeting, and (2) product targeting.

Sponsored Products—Manual Keyword Targeting

Keyword targeting allows you to choose specific keywords to add to your campaign. This can help your products appear in shopping results and product detail pages. When creating or updating a keyword campaign, you can choose from Amazon's recommended keywords, enter your own or combine both.

Amazon provides keyword recommendations, along with suggested bids. Amazon tailors these recommendations for you. It generates these keywords by blending relevant insights from across its platform; these recommendations are created as follows:

(1) First, assess which keywords performed well for you in the past; as a new seller, these will not be available. Therefore, Amazon will evaluate those which performed well across the marketplace, more broadly, for a similar product, and

(2) Second, look at what customers search for on Amazon and how often these searches translate into sales.

(3.2.1) Manual Keyword Targeting Strategies

Broad Match

This match type offers the broadest exposure, enabling you to gain impressions and drive awareness. There's no need to enter multiple versions of a keyword, as broad match includes the plural form of the keyword, related shopping queries, and other variations close to the targeted keyword. The matched search terms will contain all targeted keyword components in any order. For example, if you're advertising a "Doppler cotton sheet set", the broad match will appear against shopping queries such as "Doppler cotton sheets", "Doppler cotton sheet sets", "Blue doppler cotton sheets", and "Doppler 400-count cotton sheets"

Phrase Match

This match type is more restrictive than a broad match and will generally result in more relevant placements for your ad. It offers a balance between broad and exact matches. The matched search terms will contain all targeted keyword components in the same order. Phrase match also includes the plural form of the keyword. For example, if you're advertising a "Doppler cotton sheet set", the phrase match will appear against shopping queries such as "Doppler cotton sheet set blue", "Doppler cotton sheet sets", and "King doppler cotton sheet set."

Exact Match

This match is the most restrictive match type and tends to result in the highest conversion rates. The search terms are matched word for word (same "exact words" and in the same order) with the targeted keyword. Exact match also includes the plural form of the keyword. For example, if you're advertising a "Doppler cotton sheet set", the exact match will appear against shopping queries such as "Doppler cotton sheet set" and "Doppler cotton sheet sets."

In my 5 years of selling on Amazon—my best-performing ad strategies are:

Campaign types	**Targeting options**	**Targeting strategy**		**Best performing strategy**
Sponsored products	Automatic	Close match		Dynamic bid down only
	Manual	Keyword targeting	Phrase match	Dynamic bid down only
Sponsored brands	Manual	Keyword targeting	Broad match	Dynamic bid down only
			Phrase match	Dynamic bid up to 10%
			Exact match	Dynamic bid up to 10%

you want to use specific, best-performing keywords and
ıd optimise where they appear in the search results and
detail pages.

rwords aren't case-sensitive, so Amazon will match
se or lowercase letters in search terms;
re is a maximum limit of 10 words per keyword and 80
ers;
words can contain letters, numbers, or spaces; and
er special characters such as question marks, slashes,
quotes, ampersand/backlash are not permitted.

Sponsored Products—Manual Product Targeting

targeting is manual targeting that allows you to target products and categories relevant to the products you are ing. You can target individual products/categories, for , "women's running shoes".

her refine category targets by product attributes, such as price range, ratings, and prime shipping eligibility. When g a product, your ad will be eligible for impressions on the product's detail page and search result pages where the product appears among the top search results. There are ways to get started with product targeting: (1) use metrics ıto-targeting campaigns; (2) see "suggested" targets; and with category targeting.

ose product targeting when:

know the products or categories you want to target and king for broad reach rather than targeting specific -related keywords and:

re launching a campaign in a different country and don't rely on translations for keyword research.

advertisers who use keyword and product targeting in their products campaigns see 14.38% more impressions, 15% more d 11% more conversions compared to advertisers who use keyword only"—Amazon Internal Data, US, June 2021

Determining the right level of a manual bid is the tricky part, and this is a product of time, target ACOS, inventory levels and profit forecast. Initially, getting to the right balance is tricky, so you must set a daily budget and change the bid as needed. Allocate a higher daily budget and bid to sell more, and lower if the ad spend is too high. Naturally, your conversion will increase as you sell more and more and accumulate reviews. Your overall ACOS will decrease as your conversion rate increases.

Finding an accurate bid on specific keywords helps determine the value of advertising campaigns and the level of profit that you generate. Perform detailed reviews of your bids and their impact on sales and profitability; over a period, you will find a "sweet spot" where the additional revenue from advertising is high enough to cover your administration and advertising costs and make your startup profitable.

There is a discrepancy between what has worked for me and what Amazon recommends. Below are some recommendations from Amazon that you can try if my targeting strategies above don't work with your products:

(1) Test all three match types with different bids to help maximise your campaign performance—for example, if one of your keywords is "Doppler cotton sheet set", add it in broad, phrase and exact match and use suggested bids for each. If you manage bids at the ad group level rather than the individual keyword level, dynamic bid up and down will help you maximise performance. This is like telling the "amazon algorithm" to use its own discretion in allocating more resources to keywords that perform better—but within a budget.

(2) When setting manual bids, set your highest bid on the exact match—a lower one on the phrase match, and the lowest on the broad match. Test different match types for at least one to two weeks to gather enough data before pausing any keywords that are not performing well. You won't be bidding against yourself by adding different match types on the same keyword.

Under automatic targeting, an ad group will be an automatic ad that includes all targeting strategies: matches, closest match, loose match, substitutes and complements—to manage campaign performance. Amazon recommends using "dynamic bidding up and down" to help maximise performance, or, if you are looking to optimise based on return on ad spend "ROAS"—see below–then try a "dynamic down only" strategy.

ROAS is a metric that shows the effectiveness of an advertising campaign by measuring revenue against the ad spend. The ROAS formula is the amount of revenue from an ad campaign divided by the amount spent on the campaign itself—the higher the ROAS, the better. The formula is the opposite of ACOS in terms of numerator and denominator.

Keyword Types

You may have heard of different t including branded keywords and categ these in detail:

Branded Keywords

Branded keywords are directly associa include just the brand name, for exa well as any combination of the brand example, "KitchenSmart espresso mac your branded keyword as a brand de competitors may be bidding on themselves.

Don't bid too much for your brand much with your name at first. You wi would have searched for your brand they have had a personal recomme Shoppers searching for your products are probably willing to scroll down th find your product, so it doesn't matter outbid you.

Category Keywords

Category keywords are non-bran product/category. They can be short-t SEO chapter.

Do your Keyword Research

It can be helpful to research the descri product detail pages and explore how product's category describe their pro inspire your keyword selection. Howev time on this; take the top five sellin titles, bullet points and descriptions pattern and the similarities, includin repeated. Those will to be your ke targeting when you: (1) know what ke (2) want to have greater control over y

and (3)
drive a
produc

(1) Ke
upperc
(2) The
charact
(3) Key
(4) Ot
double

(3.2.3)

Produc
specific
advertis
exampl
Furt
brand,
targetin
targetec
targetec
several
from au
(3) start
Cho
(1) You
are loc
product
(2) You
want to
"US
sponsorec
clicks, ar
targeting

Amazon's recommendations go on and on about targeting a broad range of categories and ASINs to build brand awareness. This is a costly strategy—you must narrow it down to only a few ASINs doing well in your category. I usually target the top 10 competitors and, over time, narrow it down to the campaign's best-performing 3—5 ASINs and switching off the rest. This strategy works well when you have accumulated a few reviews, and your price is lower than the products that you are targeting. Be careful with category targeting—Amazon categories have so many product variations that you might end up targeting too many products and spending your budget on clicks from shoppers who have no intention of purchasing your product.

(3.3) Sponsored Products—Negative Targeting

Negative targeting can be completed in two parts:

(1) Negative targeting—keywords; and

(2) Negative targeting—products.

Negative targeting—keywords:

You should add the following as negative keywords: (1) low-performing keywords; and (2) search terms you don't want your ads to appear against.

Add negative keywords as both phrase and exact matches on your ads: (1) with the negative phrase option, ads won't show on shopping queries that contain the complete phrase or close variations, and (2) with negative exact option, ads won't appear on shopping queries containing the exact phrase or close variation.

You can add negative keywords for the entire campaign/ad groups. Remember, adding negative targets is not permanent—you can always remove them. However, let any changes that you make run for at least two weeks—this way, you can assess how much money the negative keywords have saved you over the period.

Negative targeting—products: You should add the following as negative products: (1) low-performing ASINs; (2) ASINs you don't want your ads to show against; and (3) non-complementary ASINs in an ad group.

For example—you're running an ad for a camera lens. Your campaign objective is for your ad to appear on complementary products, but you find it next to a non-compatible camera. By adding that camera as a negative ASIN, you can stop your ad from appearing there and help prevent paying for placements that are not relevant to your product. With product targeting, you can add a negative list of products to prevent ads from displaying on those ASINs product pages.

My best-performing campaigns are manual keyword targeted, specifically, "phrase match", with only three to four phrases.

I have tried all sorts of advertising strategies and experiments, and have lost a fair bit of money—so avoid my mistakes. I am not saying product targeting doesn't work; it's just not as effective, especially when you are starting. Therefore, allocating all your advertising budget and effort to the most efficient method makes sense. After you have mastered keyword targeting exact and phrase match and are comfortable with your ACOS ratio, you can try other advertising strategies.

Only create a few campaigns. It will take time to track which ones are performing well. At one point, I had 50+ campaigns running for only seven products, and every night, I had to review their performance—trying to keep up, adjusting bids, and updating them with the latest negative keywords was a nightmare.

Adding on to what I have already said above—if I were launching a new product today, I would:
(1) Start with a small daily budget—start with how much I want to spend each month and divide by 30. I know that I will run the risk of overspending if I don't set a daily budget. I would run automatic, "close match" ads for at least one month;
(2) Use the keywords that have had sales in the first month to create manual keyword targeting: "exact match", "phrase match" and "broad match" for three months;
(3) I will keep the automatic campaigns with a low ACOS and shut down the automated campaigns that don't work;
(4) For all campaigns I will keep the daily budget the same if they are performing well and in line with the target ACOS ratio, but I will reduce the bid. If I am desperate to report huge sales figures and with high inventory levels—and need money to pay upcoming invoices, I will increase the daily budget and increase the bids for campaigns with low ACOS;
(5) I will religiously—daily, for three months, review the campaigns' performance and add negative keywords as necessary; and
(6) From month 4 onwards, I will start reviewing once a week, for 30 minutes to an hour and add other campaign types, for example, sponsored brand videos using manual keywords.

Only add keywords that make sense, not because Amazon recommends them. Amazon has recommended some costly keywords to me. I trusted that, if it was coming from Amazon, it was "legit". Probably—yes, but Amazon also provides the same data to your competitors, so you will begin to outbid each other. I also think that the data provided is computer-generated and sent automatically. No humans are examining it to ensure there are no issues with it—if the keywords don't make sense, don't add them!

Sponsored Products—Strategic Targeting

When launching a new sponsored products campaign, you may have a variety of objectives. This might include: (1) ensuring your new product gains as much visibility as possible; (2) further increasing sales after your successful launch; and (3) looking to amplify your reach and help your brand engage with more shoppers on Amazon.

Start by defining your startup's goals

When creating a campaign, defining your main objective can help you choose your targeting method.

Think about identifying the business goals that you want to pursue for each product you sell. Take pricing, availability, and the category into account, so that you can group your products logically within your campaigns.

Next, choose your campaign strategy

Depending on your primary advertising objective, choose the strategy that meets your objective best—e.g.:

Expand*: focus on high traffic category keywords and products

Promote**: create a specific campaign to drive sales of products with specific discounts e.g. Prime member discounts.

Protect: focus on branded keywords and targeting

Conquest: target competitors' products

Upsell: use keywords geared towards higher-priced items, such as larger sizes of the product you're advertising. Use this strategy if your product has variations.

Cross-sell: target products in adjacent categories—like I said above this can be very expensive, be careful. If you decide to target other related catergories, start with a small budget.

*I use this strategy under normal circumstances, so it's "business as usual" for me. **I use this strategy when I have high levels of inventory in FCs or need money to pay off debts or creditor balances that are already due.

How to Manage and Structure Your Ads

Campaign creation—when creating campaigns, structure them in a way that makes it easier for you to monitor performance. For instance, suppose you're looking to optimise ROAS for one of your products but want to drive awareness and focus on impressions for another product. In that case, you should set up two separate ad groups within the same campaign, or two different campaigns. I always prefer separate campaigns.

Ad group name—assign an ad group name that is descriptive and meaningful to you. Ad group names must be unique within a campaign; however, you can use the same name in different campaigns.

Campaign editing—you can add new products to an ad group anytime. After saving it, you can add more ad groups to a campaign and remember to consistently keep adding on negative terms.

Targeting strategy—you should avoid mixing different strategies within the same campaign and ad group. This will also help you align and monitor performance between the advertising tactics and their impact on your overall KPIs. For instance, rate impressions or click-through rates can measure consideration and brand awareness tactics. However, conversion tactics are measured based on sales.

Products—include similar products in each ad group. Keywords, products, category targeting and bids will apply to all products within an ad group. A different bidding strategy should be in its own ad group.

Performance optimisation—optimise your campaigns regularly by applying what you have learned from your reports. You should establish benchmarks based on your goals and the historical performance of your campaigns. The ACOS is the most important KPI. Update your startup's forecasts for at least the next six months using your actual ACOS and see if you are still profitable overall. If not, you need to change your ad strategies. Starting with only two campaigns—automatic and manual—with only a few high-traffic keywords, you should not go wrong.

Ready to Start Advertising? Here's How it Works

In SC, under the main menu, click "Advertising"—"Campaigns" followed by "Create campaign"—type in your "Ad group name"—select the products you want to advertise, followed by either "Automatic" or "Manual" campaign. Decide how much you want to pay per click. This process takes about five minutes—sponsored products launch immediately, while sponsored brands, sponsored display, and stores undergo a moderation review. Based on relevance and bid, ads are shown to customers in high-visibility placements within shopping results and on product detail pages.

13 THE TRUTH ABOUT SELLING ON AMAZON

This book would not be complete without a summary of the pros and cons of selling on Amazon and how the risks of selling there can be mitigated.

Jeff Bezos's 2018 letter to Amazon shareholders delivered some important news about how far Amazon has reached into the fabric of consumer culture. Sales topped $177.9 billion in 2017, a 31% increase from $136 billion in 2016—but Amazon still has a long way to go to catch up to Walmart, which had sales of $485.9 billion in 2017. Still, the investor market was betting on Amazon's long-term dominance, with a reported market cap of $700 billion compared to $310 billion for Walmart.

In 2018, Bezos reported that Amazon had exceeded 100 million Prime members worldwide. Prime is Amazon's fee-based loyalty program that guarantees members free two-day delivery on most orders, streaming services, and access to Amazon Every Day and Prime Pantry products and other services. Considering that the U.S.—Amazon's biggest market, has 126 million households and 100 million Prime members, it is an impressive number, especially considering that they pay $120 per year for the privilege.

Bezos also reported that more than 300,000 U.S.-based small

and medium-sized enterprises ("SMEs") sell through Amazon's marketplace. More than half of all units sold on Amazon worldwide were from its third-party sellers—mostly SMEs.

With 100 million thoroughly committed Prime customers and numerous studies finding that more than half of all product searches start on Amazon, it is no wonder that so many SMEs have turned to Amazon to find new customers.

Source: 2017 – 2018 Amazon Annual Reports & Brian Deagon, "Amazon Vs. Walmart: Locking Horns In A Battle For Retail's Future (2018)".

Selling on Amazon has its advantages and disadvantages. Here is what a group of SMEs that sold or are selling on Amazon have to say—their expert opinion:

Pros	Cons
It's "fairly easy" to get started on Amazon Marketplace. Launching as a seller on Amazon is not too tricky; it's easier in some categories than others, where prospective sellers must be approved and meet specific selling requirements. "Amazon makes it easy to reach a large consumer base at scale and gives you the tools and infrastructure needed to do so," says David Heacock, CEO of FilterBuy (www. filterbuy.com), which sells replacement air filters for heating and cooling systems. "Getting started is easier than setting up your website and warehousing infrastructure. Create your product listing, send inventory to an FBA warehouse, and you are in business."	**Unscrupulous sellers can steal your detailed product listings.** Watch Ya' Mouth (www. skyimagine.com) found out about hijacking the hard way, by losing sales but still getting the bad reviews. "'Copycats gamed the Amazon system' with us, to gain the market share. They listed counterfeit products under our legit ASIN on Amazon, thus using all of our marketing to get attention to their product," shares Peter Denbigh, co-creator of Watch Ya' Mouth game. "It was a massive problem for us that we still feel the effects of, due to poor customer reviews of these counterfeit products, but the reviews show up under our legit product." This issue rarely happens now—Amazon has significantly progressed in handling counterfeits and listing hijacking through the Brand Central registry. Refer to the Branding and Trademarks chapter.

Pros	Cons
Suitable for companies selling through a unique brand and with higher profit margins Amazon Marketplace can be a good partner for companies selling under a unique brand. "Amazon helped grow our business exponentially," says Joe Jaconi, cofounder and general manager of Tech Armor (www.techarmor.com), a screen protector and mobile accessories brand. "The Amazon Marketplace is easy to use and empowers the small business to chart its destiny. The FBA program has taken the heavy lifting of logistics off our shoulders, allowing us to focus on building great products and servicing our customers." Companies that make and market their brands should have pricing control to maintain adequate margins to give Amazon their hefty commission. "If you are selling products with relatively low mark-up, it	**Con: Amazon is greedy** One 12-year veteran selling on Amazon, Adam Watson of Hollywood Mirrors (www.hollywoodmirrors.co.uk), who reported growing businesses to over $3 million a year there, has abandoned the site because its commissions are too high and the demands for free delivery cut into profit margins. Further rampant competition on Amazon forced sellers to mark down prices even further. "This resulted in our company being busy fools," Watson says. "We were turning over a large amount, but there was next to no profit at the end of it all." "There is a reason Jeff Bezos is the richest man in the world. It's from creating this perfect business model," he adds, with Amazon holding all the cards. This risk can be mitigated by selling high-margin products, and or high volumes with market depth. Refer to the Product Research chapter.

makes no sense at all to list your products on Amazon. They charge anywhere from 15-20% of the sale price in addition to the listing fees. When your margins are low, you simply can't afford to give it all to Amazon". Companies with unique brands need to be alert to the possibility of their distribution partners recognising the potential of Amazon's reach. "If business owners refuse to sell themselves on Amazon and stick with traditional distribution, eventually someone else will buy the product wholesale and sell it on Amazon themselves, keeping the profit that would otherwise be yours," says Jonathan Weber, Marathon Studios (www.marathon-studios.com) which consults with small business owners about selling on Amazon. "You'll have no way to stop them unless you control your brand on Amazon from the beginning."	

Pros	Cons
	Con: Amazon owns the customer relationship Amazon Marketplace may be a way for SMEs to sell more products to more people, but ultimately, Amazon owns the customer relationship. "You can't remarket to those customers or actively sell to them in the future. They are Amazon customers". This risk can be mitigated by building your website for the same products you sell on Amazon. Refer to the Risk Management/Website chapter.
	Con: SMEs are still responsible for customer care and feedback Whether or not companies use FBA, they are ultimately responsible for customer satisfaction. "If any customer service issues arise, you have to resolve them quickly," says Rick Lite of Stress-Free Book Marketing (www.stressfreebookmarketing.com), who works with authors. "Sellers are rated by the customers, so if you aren't ready to deal with customers, this is not the best option for you." Customer reviews are the key to unlocking success on Amazon. "As a small company located in the centre of Ohio, it took a solid three months of trial and error to find out which of our products would work on a national level," says Michael

	Russell, of Ratchet Straps (www.ratchetstraps.com), who sell tie-down hardware. "Overall, we found out reviews are key. Reply to your customers, and if they have a problem with your products, you must work with them, whether shipping them a new product, returning the old product, or whatever it ultimately takes to have the customer feeling happy and coming back. In terms of SEO and sales, the most important thing is having good reviews." He goes on to add that his company is currently doing six figures a month through Amazon.

Pros	Cons
Pro: Get with Amazon or get left behind The personal care products company Maple Holistics (www.mapleholistics.com)relies on Amazon for most of its business and is doing quite nicely, thanks to Amazon. "Amazon has helped to grow our business immeasurably. Amazon is not only the dominant force behind e-commerce right now, but behind commerce in general," says Nate Masterson, the marketing manager. "While it's important for every small business to build and maintain their retail website, you simply can't compete with the number of eyes that can find your product on Amazon." Masterson believes SMEs must get on board Amazon or get left behind. "Not only would I recommend becoming an Amazon Marketplace Partner to small businesses, but I would also argue that becoming established as an Amazon Marketplace Partner is imperative to the future success of any small business. Amazon continues to grow, and the propensity of global consumers to look to Amazon to make purchases continues to grow. Amazon is the future, and businesses should adapt or get left behind."	**Con: Forewarned is forearmed** While Amazon offers unimaginable customer reach compared to any other marketplace, including the potential for global distribution, success isn't easy or guaranteed, and, while there are many stories from small businesses that have done well on Amazon, just as many businesses have lost. "I have worked with Amazon for 12+ years and have a love-hate relationship with them," says Lite of Stress-Free Marketing. "I have made much money and enjoyed the convenience of their service, but how they treat their vendors is another issue," he continues, referring to the difficulty of resolving problems if Amazon pulls the plug on a particular merchant account. "Amazon can shut your selling account down if you infringe on their policies"—Watson of Hollywood Mirrors warns. Selling on Amazon can offer unmatched potential

	for sales if appropriately managed, and the seller can control costs to give Amazon its hefty cut. You should understand Amazon's policies and requirements to ensure your seller account is not suspended. These policies and requirements are mainly there to protect you, customers and other sellers. For further details, search "Programme Policies" in SC.

14 RISK MANAGEMENT/WEBSITE

"Brands that choose to sell on Amazon but still aspire to collect customer data may gain some information through after-sale registration, app usage, and the like. However, brands must bear in mind that when they promote their products on Amazon, they learn nothing about the consumers that visited their product page but didn't buy. They might have been able to connect with them through remarketing campaigns had they visited the company's website instead."—Harvard Business Review

One way to mitigate the risk of relying only on Amazon is by selling through your website.

Create Your Website

I created my website using Shopify. Building a website is one of the fastest ways to accelerate and develop your brand outside Amazon. Today, most business owners need a website to do some of the heavy lifting. Your startup's website builds on itself. It automates and sells. It connects with customers and promotes your products. Your website will help you increase and enable brand awareness, lead generation, customer retention, loyalty, and sales. It will thus become your "digital business home"—gone are the days when brands needed a flagship store, which they would pay an arm and leg for—the good news is that creating a website is easier than you think.

Website Builder

The fastest way to create an e-commerce website is with a website builder. An easy-to-use website maker can get you up and running fast with little effort and no coding skills. The best website builder software will:

(1) Provide templates to speed up your website creation;

(2) Let you customise website templates;

(3) Save you time and money compared to hiring a web designer or web developer;

(4) Offer a library of stock images and videos and

(5) Have a drag-and-drop design tool to make changes quickly.

Sometimes, you may need more customisation options for your website. An excellent website-building tool will also provide you with access to these. Shopify has all the above.

If you know the basics around a computer you are good to go—website builder templates are self-explanatory, and all you need to do is add photos and words—you can use your own images or choose from a pool of stock images. The choice of pictures and wording you use gives the website your personality. If you are still unsure, you can get an opinion from friends or family and make changes based on the feedback that you receive. I don't think you need a web designer at this point as all the work can be completed without prior designing experience. As far as priorities go, you should establish yourself on Amazon first, build your own website, hire a web designer if your website is not selling. You can build your website 6–12 months after you have started selling on Amazon. Test the products on Amazon first, before building a fancy website for them.

When you build a website on Shopify—you can access beautiful, mobile-responsive themes, free SSL certifications and accept payments directly on your website (with no third parties required).

Shopify is a full content management system (CMS) meaning

it enables you to create and edit your website's content. Plans start at £25 per month—at the time of print. You can try Shopify during the free trial period before making a payment. Similar CMSs include Weebly, 3dcarth, Volusion, Wix, Squarespace; and GoDaddy.

Domain Name

A domain name is like a digital address where people find you online. It gives your business credibility and helps you rank higher in searches for industry-related keywords. You can customise a domain name so it's easier for customers to remember you and find your business later. Some businesses, like (Biko—www.ilovebiko.com) an online fashion retailer, get creative with domain names. The brand uses the domain ilovebiko.com. It's relatable yet clear and puts customers in the right mindset once they arrive. When choosing a domain name, be sure to:

(1) Keep it short, brandable, and memorable;
(2) Avoid hyphens and numbers;
(3) Try to secure a top-level domain, like ".com";
(4) Check for other TLDs, like a specified country or shop; and
(5) Include SEO keywords, if possible.

Your domain name should be exactly the same as, or close to your brand name; for example, if your brand name is "Tariro", and you use it to sell leather bags, your domain name could be tariro.com. When choosing your brand name, search it on the web to ensure no one is using it. I got my domain name through Go Daddy, and it costs £7/month—at the time of print.

Layout

After you have got a domain name and web hosting set up—it will be time to choose your site's layout. Your website builder will offer themes or templates you can install in your online store. Use these templates as the starting point from which to design a basic website. Themes are typically broken down into categories. Some may be best for large product catalogues. Others are for service businesses and specific industries, like restaurants/health and beauty.

The Shopify Themes Store hosts over 70 paid and free themes, each with its styles and features. Each theme is customisable and user-friendly, allowing you to preview your storefront as you make changes.

Consider the following points when picking the perfect theme:

(1) Themes come with multiple styles—look for one that has the design aesthetic you want;

(2) The theme's built-in features—consider what you need based on your website's goals. For example, use a theme with an auto-fill search bar to ensure customers find your products easily. If you're going to highlight awards and accolades, consider a theme that has a media section;

(3) Don't choose themes based on colours or fonts—you can customise these details; and

(4) Test different themes before committing—you're never stuck with a theme. If you don't like a theme's responsive design on mobile devices, you can install a new one without recreating or changing your web pages.

I use a minimalistic Shopify theme called "Handy" with an excellent mobile phone configuration. However, this is a matter of personal taste—go with the theme you like. Some are free, and most have a one-off charge of up to US$ 350—at the time of print.

Relevant Pages

A relevant page on your website means different things depending on the products you are selling. For an e-commerce site, product pages and collection pages are necessary. For example, a restaurant owner would want landing pages for their menu and specials, real estate professionals will probably add a page to showcase their properties and a form to collect the customers' contact information.

Your website needs to do more than promote your business. It needs to build trust with visitors and help them understand

your business. The standard pages to include on your website are:
(1) Homepage—this is the entrance to your website. It'll communicate who you are and what you provide. Use the homepage to make a good impression on visitors and guide them toward actions on your site;
(2) Product pages—create pages that explain your offerings and allow shoppers to buy. You may want to create separate web pages for each product you sell;
(3) Contact page—allows people to contact you if they have questions. You can include different ways to get support/direct people to a frequently asked questions ("FAQ") page. Or create a contact form where people can fill out their information and send a message to you;
(4) FAQ page—here, you can answer common questions people have about your business and products. Consider adding the common customer questions and answers from your Amazon detailed pages to this page of your website.
(5) About page—build a page that tells your brand story and explains your business model. An "About page" helps connect with visitors and builds trust. You can also add links to your profiles across social networks and
(6) Policy pages—no matter what your business model is, there are specific legal policies you'll need to follow. For instance, you'll need a returns and shipping policy. Shopify will provide you with these templates.

You don't have to stop there—however, do not do too much too quickly. Aim to create pages that build customer trust, such as blog posts or buyer's guides, and show your offering in the best light. For instance, I have included two blog pages on my website, one for the benefits of using my products and another for how to use the products. Additional pages enable you to add relevant searchable keywords, which can boost your SEO.

A seamless payment system for your website is not negotiable. You can offer express pay options like Shop Pay, G Pay, or PayPal, or let customers pay overtime with Afterpay—Shopify and most providers offer these, including most debit and credit card payments at no extra charge.

Finally, creating a professional website for your business is the beginning, not the end. Test your website. Run a quick user experience check and ensure your products are well presented. Double-check that there are no broken links or images. Send your website to colleagues, friends, and family to ensure it loads fast and it's mobile-friendly. Then give it one last look to ensure everything looks good before you publish it—to go live!

GLOSSARY OF TERMS

ACOS—"Amazon advertising cost of sales" is a metric used to measure Amazon pay-per-click (PPC) advertising campaigns. It compares the amount spent on PPC campaigns to the amount earned, and it helps determine if your brand generated campaigns that were cost-efficient.

Ad groups—provide the ability to organize, manage, and track performance of the products within your campaign. Products placed together in an ad group share the same bids and targeting (keyword or product). Each campaign consists of one or more ad groups.

Ad spend—advertising costs.

Ads, or running ads—advertising your products on Amazon.

Amazon Launch Pad—if you have developed or invented a unique product, you can launch it on Amazon through the Amazon Launch Pad Programme. Amazon Launchpad can help supercharge your brand. The programme requires a one-year commitment. After that, you can decide to stay on the programme longer or leave. Sellers on Amazon Launchpad pay an incremental 5% referral fee and the standard category referral fee on each item sold. Refer to the chapter on FBA.

CPC— cost-per-click.

Etsy, Inc.— an American e-commerce company focused on handmade or vintage items and craft supplies. These items fall under various categories: jewellery, bags, clothing, home décor, furniture, toys, art, and tools. Items described as vintage must be at least 20 years old.

FBA—Fulfilment by Amazon. Amazon takes responsibility

for packaging, labelling, warehousing, and shipping your products from their warehouse to the customers.

Fulfilment centres ("FCs")—Amazon warehouses.

Google Market Finder—this tool can be used to quantify the scale of consumer buying power in various countries and determine the demand for your products through local monthly searches, prevalent market trends, disposable income per capita, internet users, and recommended bids when advertising those products through Google's platforms.

Google Trends—analyses the popularity of top search queries in Google Search across various regions and languages. Trends uses graphs to compare the search volume of different queries over time—use it to determine the seasonality of your products before launch.

KPI—Key performance indicator.

Keywords—are the words and phrases people use when searching for something online. For example, if you are looking for a backpack to carry your laptop to and from work or college, you might type in "laptop backpack" on Amazon or the Google search bar to find the product you are after.

MOQ—minimum order quantity.

Prime Badge—you get the Amazon Prime Badge through enrolling for FBA or Seller Fulfilled Prime ("SFP"). SFP is the Prime program that allows you to deliver directly to domestic Prime customers from your warehouse. By displaying the Prime badge, you are committing to fulfilling orders with approved Prime delivery carriers at no additional charge for Prime customers. Amazon gives you access to the proper transportation solutions to help you meet the high bar for the Prime customer experience.

Private Label—a private-label retailer sells products made by a third-party manufacturer under its own brand name.

RFQ—request for quotation

SC—Seller Central

Search terms—are often mixed up with keywords by non-SEOs (search engine optimisers). Keywords are what you use to rank for search terms. Keywords are shorter sets of words that SEOs implant into your site to draw in visitors. The many variations of those keywords which people type into search engines like Google are the search terms.

Selling Partner Support ("seller support") —Amazon's support team that's dedicated to solving sellers' queries.

SERP—stands for "search engine results page." The Amazon SERP shows results to customers after they complete a product search on Amazon. To help boost product rankings on the SERP, optimise your Amazon product listings using the tools in the SEO chapter.

Shopify Inc.—is a Canadian multinational e-commerce company headquartered in Ottawa, Ontario. Shopify is the name of its proprietary e-commerce platform for online stores and retail point-of-sale systems. The Shopify platform offers online retailers a suite of services including payments, marketing, shipping and customer engagement tools.

SKU—"stock-keeping unit codes"— are a combination of letters and numbers that are created for the identification of a specific product.

SMEs—Small and medium-sized enterprises.

SSL certificate—a bit of code on your web server that provides security for online communications. When a web browser contacts your secured website, the SSL certificate enables an encrypted connection. It's kind of like sealing a letter in an envelope before sending it through the mail.

Tees—t-shirts.

QC—Quality control.

NOTES

10 advantages of setting up a limited company – (2022). Available at: https://www.bytestart.co.uk/limited-company-advantages.

How to Start Selling on Amazon UK - A Beginner's Guide (no date). Available at: https://sell.amazon.co.uk/sell-online/beginners-guide?ref_=sduk_soa_tbg_n.

Government Digital Service (2017) Estimate your Income Tax for the current year. Available at: https://www.gov.uk/estimate-income-tax.

Government Digital Service (2014) Set up a private limited company. Available at : https://www.gov.uk/limited-company-formation/register-your-company.

Government Digital Service (2017b) Estimate your Income Tax for the current year. Available at: https://www.gov.uk/estimate-income-tax.

Amazon Fulfilment UK - Free Shipping, Storage & Returns (no date). Available at : https://sell.amazon.co.uk/fulfil?ref_=sduk_soa_fullfil_n.

Fabregas, K. (2022) How to Find Products to Sell on Amazon. Available at : https://www.nerdwallet.com/article/small-business/how-to-find-products-to-sell-on-amazon.

Heegomn Waterproof Digital Camera for Children, Full HD 1080P, 8x Digital Zoom, 16MP Underwater Cam for Teenagers/Beginners (Red): Amazon.co.uk: Electronics & Photo (no date). Available at : https://www.amazon.co.uk/Heegomn-Waterproof-Underwater-Teenagers-

Beginners/dp/B0924GHM29/ref=sr_1_5?crid=3PV21MN7O30 VN.

FBA Small & Light - Fulfilment Service by Amazon UK (no date). Available at : https://sell.amazon.co.uk/fulfilment-by-amazon/fba-small-and-light.

The Economist (2020) The secret to a perfect brand name. Available at : https://www.economist.com/1843/2020/02/18/the-secret-to-a-perfect-brand-name.

Cristea, M.-A. (2021) 6 Sustainable Packaging Tips for Overseas Products. Available at : https://business-review.eu/sustainability/6-sustainable-packaging-tips-for-overseas-products-222703.

99designs (no date). The importance of branding: why branding matters. Available at : https://99designs.co.uk/blog/logo-branding/importance-of-branding/.

Matt Voss (2020) How to publish a book on Amazon - A best sellers guide to self-publishing, formatting, and marketing using Amazon ads.

Pinterest (2022) Image available at: https://www.pinterest.co.uk/pin/227291731002378444/

Amazon FBA - Let Amazon Pick, Pack, and Ship Your Orders (no date). Available at : https://sell.amazon.co.uk/fulfilment-by-amazon.

Amazon UK Seller Fee Calculator - Sell on Amazon Fees (no date). Available at: https://sell.amazon.co.uk/pricing.

Amazon UK Seller Fee Calculator - Sell on Amazon Fees (no date b). Available at : https://sell.amazon.co.uk/pricing?ref_=sduk_soa_priov_n.

Amazon Sign In (no date). Available at: https://sellercentral.amazon.co.uk:443/ap/signin?openid.return_to=https%3A%2F%2Fsellercentral.amazon.co.uk%2Fhelp%2Fhub%2Freference%2F200612770%3Fref%3Defph_200612770_cont_201074400&openid.identity=http%3A%2F%2Fspecs.openid.net%2Fauth%2F2.0%2Fidentifier_select&openid.assoc_handle=sc_uk_amazon_v2&openid.mode=checkid_setup&openid.claimed_id=http%3A%2F%2Fspecs.openid.net%2Fauth%2F2.0%2Fid

entifier_select&openid.ns=http%3A%2F%2Fspecs.openid.net%2Fauth%2F2.0&mons_redirect=sign_in&ssoResponse=eyJ6aXAiOiJERUYiLCJlbmMiOiJBMjU2R0NNIiwiYWxnIjoiQTI1NktXIn0.rCMyfHf8BhBn4mBauv4J1GFT19kAdOu1VQCYjsukN7l-O1ZqSPHumQ.mRqfFJLiNuXwoO_U.6_-d53ZSo_OpR0ASOevlk6zPT3tX5C8v9eNF_YVlKq5LYLUCs9T966WrIYLpfJSXtby9Z5vLRD3POK-oKin_2eofMvVN5kl53b9dyZP9s0jnce9JIOCT7QPydvCRlOpfdd0DLCSRIldOaty4g6kIxjkgCX5RBglnypF_v2-9RkS2FheXlkjzkgTXO9KCri8g4UuqPXbz.OfaZ6H-NbXPscarL7HWzmw.

Multi-Channel Fulfilment (MCF) - How It Works | Amazon UK (no date). Available at : https://sell.amazon.co.uk/fulfilment-by-amazon/fba-multi-channel?ref_=sduk_fba_pricing_mcf_b.

Sell Online with Amazon UK - Become an Amazon Seller Today (no date). Available at: https://sell.amazon.co.uk/sell-online.

Amazon Brand Protection Report (no date). Available at: https://brandservices.amazon.co.uk/progressreport.

Deliverr (D) (2022) What is the Amazon brand registry and how does it work? Available at: https://deliverr.com/blog/amazon-brand-registry/

Ali, M. (2022) How to Source Products to Sell on Amazon in 2022 and beyond! Available at : https://www.zonguru.com/blog/how-to-source-products-to-sell-on-amazon.

Brian Connolly (2022) How to Buy on Alibaba and Sell on Amazon. Available at : https://www.junglescout.com/blog/alibaba-to-amazon-fba/.

Alibaba.com (no date) Gold Supplier. Available at: https://www.alibaba.com/help/gold_supplier.html?spm=a2700.shop_plser.88.1.46c03403dP9VLA

Alibaba.com (no date) Introducing Verified Suppliers. Available at: https://fuwu.alibaba.com/page/verifiedsuppliers.htm?spm=a2700.galleryofferlist.normal_offer.3.a0bc3f84Fxp8Yb

Sell Online with Amazon UK - Become an Amazon Seller

Today (no date b). Available at : https://sell.amazon.co.uk/sell-online?ref_=asuk_soa_rd.

Leon, C. (2020) The Amazon Flywheel Concept, The Virtuous Cycle. Available at : https://www.charlesleon.uk/blog/the-amazon-flywheel-concept-the-virtuous-cycle1392020.

Why Cultivating a Growth Mindset Can Boost Your Success (2022). Available at : https://www.verywellmind.com/what-is-a-mindset-2795025.

Automate pricing: Adjust pricing quickly and automatically (no date). Available at: https://sell.amazon.com/tools/automate-pricing.

Quaker, D. (2022) Amazon SEO: How to Optimize Your Product Listings (Step-by-Step Guide) - Tips, info, and stories about selling in Amazon stores. Whether you're just getting started selling online or building an ecommerce empire, the Amazon Selling Partner blog features articles to help you get there. Available at : https://sell.amazon.com/blog/getting-started/amazon-seo-to-optimize-product-listings.

Amazon (no date). Available at: https://sellercentral.amazon.com/help/hub/reference/external/G202059240?ref_=sdus_blog_seo_xscus_G202059240.

Grow Online Sales with Amazon | Perfect Launch Program (no date). Available at: https://sell.amazon.com/grow.

Amazon Launchpad - Accelerated Growth for Unique Startups (no date). Available at : https://sell.amazon.co.uk/programmes/launchpad/apply?ld=SEUKALPLGN22AdGog_15571306253_130667539426_kwd-301162911508_p_569629471841_c_asret_.

Grow Your Business with Amazon Launchpad in the UK (no date). Available at : https://sell.amazon.co.uk/programmes/launchpad?ref_=sduk_soa_pr_launch_launch_f.

Government Digital Service (2014a) Register a trademark. Available at : https://www.gov.uk/how-to-register-a-trade-mark.

Amazon Brand Registry: Eligibility, Enrollment, and Access (no date). Available at: https://brandservices.amazon.co.uk/brandregistry/eligibility.

Grow Your Business Online in UK - Over £40K in Potential Benefits (no date). Available at : https://sell.amazon.co.uk/grow?ref_=sduk_soa_growwte_n.

Sell on Amazon UK & Uplift your Online Selling Experience (no date). Available at: https://sell.amazon.co.uk/.

Guidelines and Acceptance Policies: Restricted Content, Products and Services (no date). Available at : https://advertising.amazon.com/resources/ad-policy/creative-acceptance/restricted-content-products-services?ref_=a20m_us_spcs_cap_spcs_cap7.

Amazon Advertising | Increase your ecommerce channel visibility and sales (no date). Available at: https://sell.amazon.com/advertising.

Sponsored Products - Help increase product sales (no date). Available at : https://advertising.amazon.com/solutions/products/sponsored-products?ref_=a20m_us_lbr_gd_bos_intro_sp.

What is CPC (cost per click)? How PPC advertising works (2022). Available at: https://advertising.amazon.com/library/guides/cost-per-click?ref_=a20m_us_p_sp_txt_lbr_gd_cpc.

A guide to targeting with Amazon Ads' Sponsored Products (2022). Available at : https://advertising.amazon.com/en-gb/library/guides/targeting-with-sponsored-products/?ref_=a20m_us_libr.

Amazon.co.uk: Low Prices in Electronics, Books, Sports Equipment & more (no date). Available at : https://www.amazon.co.uk/ref=ap_frn_logo.

Course Hero, Inc. (no date). Packaging. Available at: https://www.coursehero.com/study-guides/boundless-marketing/packaging/

Just a moment... (no date b). Available at : https://www.junglescout.com/blog/fba-shipping-checklist/?s=shipping+from+china.

Danziger, P. (2018) Thinking of Selling on Amazon Marketplace? Here Are The Pros And Cons. Available at: https://www.forbes.com/sites/pamdanziger/2018/04/27/pros-and-cons-of-amazon-marketplace-for-small-and-mid-sized-businesses/?sh=60eff4726867.

What is an SSL Certificate? | SSL FAQs | Thawte®. (n.d.). https://www.thawte.com/resources/getting-started/ssl-faq/#:~:text=An%20SSL%20certificate%20is%20a,sending%20it%20through%20the%20mail.

Rogers, A. (2022) 21 Real Ways to Increase Website Traffic in 2023. Available at: https://www.shopify.com/uk/blog/how-to-increase-website-traffic.

Wikipedia contributors (2022) Shopify. Available at: https://en.wikipedia.org/wiki/Shopify.

Firestone, E.S.A. \U0026 C.C. (2022) How to Build a website: A Beginner's Guide (+Video 2023). Available at: https://www.shopify.com/uk/blog/build-a-website.

The Economist. (2017, October 23). Stores are being hit by online retailing. https://www.economist.com/special-report/2017/10/26/stores-are-being-hit-by-online-retailing

Israeli, A. (2022, August 17). Should Your Company Sell on Amazon? Harvard Business Review. https://hbr.org/2022/09/should-your-company-sell-on-amazon

What Is a Stock Keeping Unit (SKU)? Definition and Guide. (2022, November 11). Shopify. https://www.shopify.com/uk/blog/what-is-a-stock-keeping-unit

Backlinko. (2021, November 18). Backlinko. https://backlinko.com/seo-copywriting

BreadcrumbList - Schema.org Type. (n.d.). https://schema.org/BreadcrumbList#:~:text=A%20BreadcrumbList%20is%20an%20ItemListthe%20items%20in%20a%20BreadcrumbList.

Design beautiful product packaging in 2023 to boost loyalty. (2022, March 10). Shopify. https://www.shopify.com/uk/blog/ecommerce-packaging

Brian Deagon. Amazon Vs. Walmart: Locking Horns In A Battle For Retail's Future (2018) Available at: https://www.investors.com/news/technology/walmart-vs-amazon-retail-stores-e-commerce/

INDEX